Living Through History

NAZI GERMANY

RICHARD TAMES

Batsford Academic and Educational
London

Cover pictures

The colour photograph on the front cover shows Nazi supporters at the Nuremberg rally (Bundesarchiv). The two black and white photographs show a young German boy in his Hitler Youth uniform (Imperial War Museum) and children in a concentration camp (Novosti Press Agency).

ACKNOWLEDGMENTS

The Author and Publisher would like to thank the following individuals and organizations for their kind permission to reproduce copyright material: Archiv der Bekennenden Kirche for figures 56, 57 and 58; Bundesarchiv for figure 25; Collins and SCM Press for figures 54 and 55 from *Bonhoeffer* by Eberherd Bethge; Imperial War Museum for the frontispiece and figures 3, 5, 9, 10, 11, 12, 18, 20, 22, 26, 29, 30, 31, 32, 51, 60 and 62; Institute of Contemporary History and Wiener Library Limited for figures 6, 7, 8, 13, 14, 16, 17, 19, 24, 27, 28, 38, 39, 40, 43, 46, 47, 63 and 64; Ilse Koehn for figure 59 from *Mischling Second Degree* (Hamish Hamilton, 1977) and for extracts from the same volume; Macmillan Press for extracts from *A Documentary History of Western Civilization* (Eugene C. Black and Leonard W. Levy, eds.); Novosti Press Agency for figure 48; People's Press for figure 49 from *One Life Is Not Enough*, by Lore Wolf; Leni Riefenstahl for figures 33, 36 and 37; Search Press for figures 44 and 45 from *The Bird Has No Wings* by Peter Schwiefert and for extracts from the same volume; The Speer Archive for figures 21 and 23; John Topham Picture Library for figures 1, 2, 34, 35 and 61; Ullstein Picture Service for figures 15 and 41.

Typeset by Tek-Art Ltd, West Wickham, Kent
Printed in Great Britain by
R.J. Acford Ltd
Chichester, Sussex
for the publishers
Batsford Academic and Educational,
an imprint of B.T. Batsford Ltd,
4 Fitzhardinge Street,
London W1H 0AH

ISBN 0 7134 3538 0

Frontispiece *Father of the Nation? Hitler with youthful admirers, symbolizing innocence, trust and Germany's new future.*

CONTENTS

THE
ILLUSTRATIONS

NAZI GERMANY

"We have no scruples . . . we are barbarians. We want to be barbarians. It is an honourable title." Adolf Hitler

How could a man like Hitler have become the leader of the most highly educated and technologically advanced nation in Europe? Germany – a country famed for her philosophers, her poets and her musicians.

Some historians see the roots of Nazism lying deep in German history. For centuries German knights fought pagan Slavs, pushing German territories eastward and spreading Christianity by the sword. The Nazi conquest

1 Man of destiny. A sketch of Hitler in April 1932, suggesting his visionary qualities.

of eastern Europe and the Soviet Union could, therefore, be seen as a re-enactment of this ancient struggle, justified in the twentieth century as a fight to protect Europe from Communism rather than from paganism. Other historians point to the long-standing prejudice against the Jews, both in Germany and throughout eastern Europe where, from the time of the Crusades to the 1880s, they suffered from repeated pogroms (massacres). The Nazis, in other words, did not have to invent anti-Semitism, merely to organize it. Another theme of German history has been the power of the military over civilian authorities, especially in Prussia, a state in which society was organized to serve the army rather than vice versa. Prussia's wars against her neighbours – Denmark, Austria and France – led to annexations of parts of their territories and the creation of a united Germany in 1871, just before Hitler's birth in 1889. Hitler noted in *Mein Kampf* (*My Struggle*) that the only lessons he enjoyed at school were history lessons about Germany's wars, and his favourite reading-matter was illustrated magazines about the Franco-Prussian war of 1870–1.

Other historians have looked at the more immediate events behind the rise of Nazism and Hitler's takeover of power in January 1933: there was the shock of defeat in the Great War, although no enemy soldier stood on German soil; the chaos which followed the surrender, with the flight of the Kaiser, attempts to set up Soviets in various cities and bloody street-fighting between Communists and "Freikorps" of unemployed ex-soldiers; the shame of the Versailles Treaty which forced Germany to acknowledge her "guilt" in starting the war and to accept the loss of her colonies, her navy and most of her army; and the legend of the "Dolchstoss" ("stab in the back"), which blamed the "November Criminals", the politicians who signed the treaty on Germany's behalf, betraying both

2 "Germans! Who should lead? Who should be our captain?" The back page of *Ostaria*, an early (1922) racialist magazine. The crusader poses a choice between a noble, blonde figure and a swarthy, brutal-looking one.

her honour and her interests. The weaknesses of the Weimar Republic (the democratic regime of 1919-33) have also been blamed: the endless, fruitless squabbling of party politicians; the economic uncertainties created by massive inflation and mass unemployment; the failure to win the allegiance of powerful interests like the army and big business. Finally, there are those historians who see in Hitler himself the best explanation of the appeal of Nazism: his powers of oratory and the close correspondence between his own intense racism, his fanatical nationalism and his sense of personal destiny and the frustrations and

3 SA – Service for friendship, fortitude and strength.

longings of the crisis-ridden people of Germany. Hitler's personality, and the party and programme he created, seemed to many Germans to offer both an explanation of the nation's problems and the means to their solution.

As German democracy faltered, so the Nazis gained in strength – from 27,000 party members in 1925 to 176,000 in 1929, 806,000 in 1931 and almost two million a year later, on the eve of Hitler's accession to power. As Nazi party membership grew, so did Nazi voting strength, though less steadily because there were still other nationalist parties that could attract potential Nazi voters. The Nazis entered the Reichstag, (the German Parliament) democratically and legally, but their objective was to destroy both democracy and the rule of law. Goebbels himself declared in 1928:

We are entering the Reichstag in order that we may arm ourselves with the weapons of democracy from its arsenal. We shall become Reichstag deputies in order that the Weimar ideology should itself help us to destroy it.

The Nazi view of law was summed up by Wilhelm Frick (Minister of the Interior 1933-43): "Right is whatever benefits the German people, wrong is whatever harms them." It was, of course, to be left to the Nazi party to decide what was "benefit" and what was "harm".

From a mere 12 seats in 1928, the Nazis increased their parliamentary strength to 107 in 1930 and became the largest single party, with 230 seats, in 1932, though even in 1933, with 288 seats, they were unable to command an absolute majority in their own right. But, after Hitler's appointment as Chancellor (30 January 1933) and the burning down of the Reichstag, parliamentary limits on his authority were swept aside by the passing of an "Enabling Law" which gave him dictatorial powers for four years. The Reichstag building had been reduced to a shell, the Reichstag as an institution meant little more. Four years was quite long enough for the Nazis to carry out their "revolution from above", using the powers of government and police to crush all opposition to their rule.

The Nazi revolution was a political revolution. It decisively changed Germany from a constitutional democracy into a totalitarian state in which decision-making was based on the "Führerprinzip" (the leader principle) and the citizen, rather than having guaranteed rights and a private life outside the control of the government, was reduced to the level of a mere cell in the mighty body of the "Volk" (the German people).

In cultural terms, also, the Nazis attempted a revolution, suppressing what they considered to be "decadent" art and driving into exile Germany's greatest modern

◁ **4** Albert Einstein (1879-1955). Nobel Prize winner, whose books were publicly burnt in May 1933. Like many other exiles from Nazism he made his home in America.

novelist, Thomas Mann, her greatest scientist, Albert Einstein, and celebrated artists like Grosz and Kandinsky.

Socially, the Nazi takeover also produced a revolution as thousands of opportunists jumped on to the Nazi bandwagon, and the cultured and influential Jewish minority was forced out of positions of authority and influence.

Economically, the transformation of Germany was no less striking. Unemployment was cut from six million to less than one million in four years. National output doubled between 1932 and 1937. But, significantly, big business, like the army, was shielded from the

5 "Aryan maidens", intended as the mothers of new Germany.

radicals who still took the socialist aspects of "National Socialism" seriously. Hitler would allow nothing to damage Germany's war-making power. So industry and the army were built up for the task assigned to them by the Nazi plan: the establishment of a Greater Germany as the dominant power of a "New Order" based on "Aryan" supremacy. The attempt to create that "New Order" was to cost Germany some five million dead, the rest of the world perhaps ten times that number.

SERVANTS OF THE FÜHRER

According to Goering:

When a decision has to be taken, none of us count for more than the stones on which we are standing. It is the Führer alone who decides.

One man may make all the important decisions. But he cannot carry them all out. Hitler ruled by lies and terror but even he needed servants, great and small, to translate the will to deceive and oppress into actual headlines, broadcasts, beatings and executions. Some of Hitler's comrades, like Ernst Röhm, commander of the SA (the Nazis' private army), were thugs of low intelligence; brutal and perverted. Others, like Alfred Rosenberg, who posed as the philosopher of Nazism, were frustrated intellectuals. Hess, the faithful secretary to whom Hitler dictated *Mein Kampf*, the Bible of the Nazi movement, was distinguished by his dog-like devotion to the Führer. Bormann and Frick made themselves indispensible through their mastery of the state and party bureaucracies. As for the military, though some, like General Keitel and Admiral Raeder, were convinced Nazis, most regarded the movement and its leader with contempt. But most were also prepared to close their eyes to its barbarism, either for motives of supposed patriotism or in the interests of their own careers. It would be easy to portray the Nazi leaders as mere political gangsters, without brains or moral standards, who simply obeyed Hitler's orders without question. But, as the historian A.J.P. Taylor has warned (*The Origins of the Second World War*, second edition, Penguin 1963, pp. 26-7):

Little can be discovered so long as we go on attributing everything that happened to

6 Frontispiece of Hitler's *Mein Kampf* (*My Struggle*), written during his imprisonment after the failure of the 1923 Munich *putsch*.

Hitler. . . . He would have counted for nothing without the support and co-operation of the German people. It seems to be believed nowadays that Hitler did everything himself, even driving the trains and filling the gas chambers unaided. This was not so. . . . Thousands, many hundred thousand, Germans carried out his evil orders without qualm or question.

Some of Hitler's collaborators like Robert Ley, the labour leader (see pp. 25-9), were "Alte Kämpfer" ("old fighters"), survivors of the "Kampfzeit" ("time of struggle"), the days of obscurity, persecution and street-fighting, which laid the foundations of Nazism as a movement and a myth. Others, like Heydrich and Speer (see pp. 19-25), were ambitious technicians attracted by the new opportunities opened up by the Nazis' challenge to the old, privileged classes.

One of Hitler's favourite pastimes was to reminisce about old times with party veterans, but he did not hesitate to arrange the murder of those, like Ernst Röhm and Gregor Strasser, who threatened his own personal power, or to let others, like Streicher, Rosenberg and Goering, decline into virtual powerlessness after they had served their purpose or failed him. Equally, it must be remembered that, in his later years, as Hitler's obsession with the details of military operations and unwillingness to listen to any contrary argument led him further into a twilight world of illusion, he became to some extent manipulated by his most devoted associates, like his secretary, Martin Bormann, who virtually controlled his daily diary, and Joseph Goebbels, who became his major link with the German people. And it was Goebbels himself who pronounced the most appropriate judgment upon them all:

History will remember us as the greatest statesmen of all times or as her greatest criminals.

Joseph Goebbels (1897-1945)

Like many other Germans of his generation, Joseph Goebbels found in Nazism and in Hitler the cause and the leader which would transform his life from failure to success. Goebbels was born in 1897, the son of a factory clerk from the Rhineland, and was brought up in a strict Catholic atmosphere. Stricken by polio in his childhood, he was intended for the Church by his devout parents. Physically weak and undersized, conventional, well-mannered and clever, Goebbels was to identify strongly with the ideal figure of the Nazi hero who was his complete opposite – strong, blond, pagan, a creature of instinct rather than calculation, with nothing but contempt for the petty rules of polite society.

Rejected for military service in the Great War on account of his crippled foot, Goebbels studied history and literature and graduated from the prestigious University of Heidelberg in 1920. In 1922 he joined the Nazi party after hearing Hitler speak at a mass rally. By 1925 he was business manager of the party in the Rühr, the heartland of industrial Germany. Working-class by background, Goebbels at first supported the socialist aspects of "National Socialism", seeing Soviet Russia as "Germany's natural ally against the devilish temptations and corruptions of the West". At the 1926 party conference he sponsored a programme of radical reforms and called for the expulsion from the party of "petty-bourgeois Adolf Hitler". But Hitler's personal authority was too great for Goebbels to challenge. So Goebbels switched sides. And was rewarded with the appointment of "Gauleiter" (regional head of the Nazi organization) for Berlin, the nation's capital and a city with a strong Communist presence. Within months of taking over he had doubled the party's membership in the city.

Goebbels' political aims were very straightforward:

Whoever can conquer the street will one day conquer the state, for every form of power politics and any dictatorially run state has its roots in the street.

But how to capture power in the streets? Goebbels' method was simple rather than subtle. By marching his followers through "Red" districts, he provoked fights with the Communists and built up a reputation for the Nazis as defender of "order" against the "Red Menace". In 1927 he founded and edited his own weekly newspaper *Der Angriff* (*The Attack*). The murder of Horst Wessel, a Nazi "Stormtrooper" and petty criminal, gave him a ready-made martyr, the hero of the "Horst Wessel Lied" (Horst Wessel song), which was to become almost a second national anthem for Germany under the Nazis. In 1928 Goebbels was elected to the Reichstag as a Nazi deputy.

8 ". . . he has intelligence and the gift of oratory. I have never regretted giving him the powers he asked for" Adolf Hitler 24 June, 1942.

Hitler was greatly impressed by Goebbels' success in establishing a powerful Nazi presence in Berlin. In 1929 he appointed him Reich Propaganda Leader. Goebbels responded by organizing street riots which forced cinemas to stop showing the anti-war film *All Quiet on the Western Front* and, far more importantly, by helping to organize the 1932 election campaign which brought Hitler to the centre of the political stage in Germany's hour of crisis.

Goebbels was rewarded on 13 March 1933 with the position of Reich Minister for Public Enlightenment and Propaganda. At the age of 35 he was the youngest minister in the modern history of Germany. Two months after his appointment he organized a public burning of books by Jewish, Marxist and other authors whose works were contrary to Nazi ideas.

9 Book burning. Students and SA men "cleanse" the libraries.

Propaganda was, of course, destined to play a central role in the creation of the Nazi state. Hitler had written extensively on the importance of propaganda in *Mein Kampf*:

The art of propaganda consists precisely in being able to awaken the imagination of the public through an appeal to their feelings. . . . Propaganda must not investigate the truth objectively but it must present only that aspect of the truth which favours its own side.

Goebbels understood this very well and, indeed, admitted quite candidly in private that:

Any person with the slightest spark of honour left in him will take good care in future not to become a journalist.

Frustrated by rivals like Otto Dietrich and Max Amann in his attempts to establish total personal control over the press and publishing, Goebbels swiftly made himself master of the new electric media – wireless (radio) and cinema. Radio gave Goebbels direct access to the home, the café and the street. Whilst Hitler had no equal before a live audience, Goebbels outshone even the Führer on the air; and, unlike his master, he spoke in a voice which betrayed his education – and even a touch of humour, qualities which Hitler decidedly lacked. At times, Goebbels' tone was deliberately elevated, as when he told an audience that:

We Germans, under the leadership of Adolf Hitler, take on us a new world mission. The fight has begun for fatherland, liberty, honour, family and religion.

But Goebbels also realized that successful propaganda could not rely on politics and high culture all the time. People wanted jokes and cartoons as well as slogans and serious music. So he used light entertainment and films to build up the idea of the superiority of everything German and of the infallible wisdom of Adolf Hitler. Goebbels managed to give immense emotional power to slogans such as "Der Führer ist Sieg" (The Leader is Victory) which were, in themselves, quite meaningless. Indeed, Goebbels' great achievement as a propagandist was to create an enduring image of Hitler as the sincere, righteous, trustworthy leader, standing head and shoulders above the gang of ambitious and greedy men who competed for his favours. This meant that even in the last stages of the war, when many German soldiers were utterly disillusioned with the cruelties and injustices of the Nazi leadership, most of them still regarded the Führer himself with respect and even affection.

Goebbels worked his staff hard, but no harder than he worked himself. He found his relaxation in luxury and love affairs. This did not make him popular with ordinary people; but he never sought popularity – only power.

10 Propaganda poster calling for a "Yes" vote in the plebiscite to approve the re-integration of Austria into the Reich.

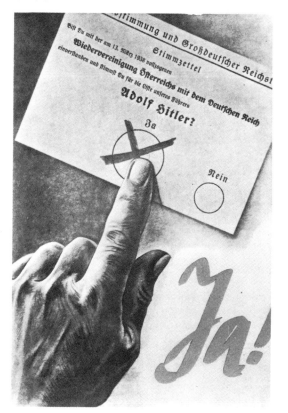

However, despite his enormous influence on Germany's cultural life and his ability to organize conferences, exhibitions and rallies, he was constantly being up-staged by other Nazi leaders who carried more weight with Hitler because they were more closely involved with the business of preparing for, or actually fighting, the war. Then, as the war situation got worse, it became more and more important to build up the morale of the German people and Goebbels' influence grew correspondingly greater. On 18 February 1943 he made a speech in the Berlin Sportpalast which drove his carefully selected audience to a frenzied demand for "total war". But it was more than a year before Goebbels won his final reward for his loyalty to the Führer's cause.

In July 1944, a week after the attempt on Hitler's life (and the attempted coup d'état in Berlin which Goebbels himself helped to scotch), the Reich Minister for Public Enlightenment and Propaganda – was appointed to the specially created post of Reich Commissioner for Total Mobilization. And, as Hitler withdrew more and more from public life to devote himself obsessively to matters of strategy, so Goebbels stepped forward to take his place at the microphone.

In the last year of the war Goebbels achieved

11 Goebbels addresses a carefully stage-managed mass meeting.

Adolf Hitler ist der Sieg!

fulfilment as the passionate champion of a doomed cause. Harking back to Germany's great war of liberation against Napoleon, he called upon an exhausted nation with historic words:

Now People rise
And Storm break loose!

"Resistance at all costs" was Goebbels' last proclamation. It was a fitting epitaph. Named Chancellor in Hitler's will, he followed his master's example by committing suicide, having first poisoned his six children and shot his wife. He was the only high-ranking Nazi leader to die with Hitler in his Berlin bunker. His last words were: "When we depart, let the earth tremble." They were suitably theatrical.

Heinrich Himmler (1900-45)

Engraved on the dagger carried by every member of the SS ("Schutz-Staffel", Hitler's personal bodyguard) was its motto: "Meine Ehre heisst Treue" ("Loyalty is my Honour"). Unquestioning obedience, no matter what the order, was the most essential quality required of the "supermen" of the Nazis' "New Order". Few people can have looked less like a superman than Heinrich Himmler, head of the SS, head of the Gestapo, the most feared man in Europe.

Born in 1900, the son of a strict Catholic Bavarian schoolmaster, Himmler served briefly as an officer cadet at the end of the Great War, studied for a diploma in agriculture, joined a para-military nationalist organization and took part in the failed "Putsch" of 1923 in which Hitler prematurely attempted to seize power.

In 1929 Himmler was given command of the SS. By 1933 Himmler had expanded its membership from 200 picked men to more than 50,000, but there was no decline in the physical standards required for entry. Until 1936 even a filling in a tooth was enough to keep a man out. After that, the continuing expansion of the organization and its demand for experts as well as would-be warriors, did lead to a lowering of the physical requirements for entry. But Himmler went much further than this in his efforts to make the SS

altogether different from the three-million-strong SA ("Sturm Abteilung", the storm troops who had helped the Nazis win power on the streets), and rituals mixing the ceremonies

13 "I see in Himmler our Ignatius de Loyola. With intelligence and obstinacy, against wind and tide, he formed the SS." Adolf Hitler 3 January, 1942.

of pagan warriors and medieval knights were invented to set the SS apart.

When Hitler took power in 1933, Himmler was put in charge of the police in Munich, capital of his native Bavaria. In the same year he established the first concentration camp at Dachau. By April 1934 he was effectively in charge of every police force in Germany. Two months later he took the leading part in organizing the "Night of the Long Knives" (also known as the "Blood Purge"). On 30 June 1934, under cover of pretending to smash a plot against Hitler, he was able to arrange the murder of Ernst Röhm and other SA leaders as well as several generals, such as von Schleicher, who were threatening to be troublesome to the new regime. In a speech given in Berlin on 13 July 1934, Hitler announced that 61 "plotters" had been shot, a further 13 had died resisting arrest and three had committed suicide. In fact, at least 150 SA leaders had been killed and later historians have claimed that the figure may have been more than 1000. Whatever the truth, this bloody incident served notice to all would-be opponents of the new regime that opposition would come at a high price.

Having thus disposed of the main rivals to his own power, Himmler continued to expand his personal empire. An efficient and hard-working administrator, he was able to concentrate all political, criminal and security police forces, including the Gestapo, under his supreme authority by 1936. In this task he was greatly assisted by his own chosen assistent, Reinhard Heydrich (see pp. 19-21).

If one side of Himmler was calculating and ruthless, the other was mystical and romantic. He was fascinated by hypnotism, the occult, herbal medicine, German folklore and the ancient history of the Germans. In 1936, for instance, he organized elaborate celebrations to mark the thousandth anniversary of the death of Henry the Fowler, the Saxon king who led the German advance eastward against the Slavs. Himmler saw in this shadowy figure an inspiration for the Nazis' own "racial mission" which necessarily involved:

the struggle for the extermination of any sub-humans all over the world who are in league against Germany, which is the nucleus of the Nordic race; against Germany, nucleus of the German nations, against Germany the custodian of human culture. . .

Himmler built up the SS to carry out the Nazi racial mission. This mission had both its negative aspect – the mass-murder of Jews, Slavs and other non-Aryans, within Germany and in the conquered territories of the east, and its positive aspect – the selection and training of an aristocracy of blond supermen who would both create and preside over the "New Order" and represent, in themselves, its finest achievement. Like the Teutonic Knights who had spread Christianity by the sword in the Middle Ages, Himmler's SS was to express its elite character by means of elaborate rituals, splendid uniforms and oaths of personal loyalty to its leaders.

In October 1939 the Führer appointed Himmler as Reich Commissioner for the Strengthening of Germandom, with absolute authority over that part of conquered Poland which was to be annexed to Germany. "Strengthening of Germandom" meant, in practice, expelling one million Poles and 300,000 Jews and replacing them with people of German descent from the Baltic countries and other parts of Poland. Himmler's success in carrying out this brutal transfer of populations encouraged Hitler to entrust "der treue Heinrich" (loyal Henry) with carrying out the "Final Solution" of the "Jewish Question", although Himmler himself had once written in a memorandum that the idea of actually exterminating all Jews was "bolshevik . . . un-German and impractical". But, in 1941, Himmler accepted his "historic duty to carry it out by all means", although he later confessed at a secret SS leaders' conference:

the execution of this difficult command which the Führer had laid upon my shoulders [is] the heaviest task that has ever been imposed on me.

Physically nauseated by the sight of killing, the Reichsführer SS nevertheless proceeded

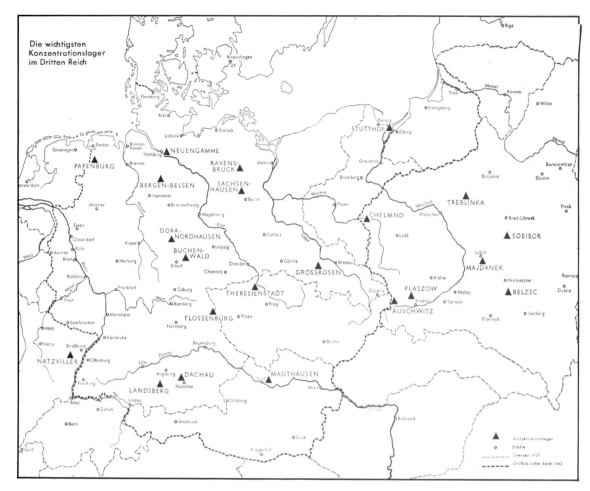

14 Major concentration camps of "Greater Germany".

with the organizing of the systematic shooting, hanging, gassing and burning of more than six million Jews, gypsies, Slavs, Communists, Catholics and other "Untermenschen" ("sub-humans"). From time to time he found it necessary to remind his SS comrades of the essential nobility of their work, as in a speech given to SS leaders at Poznan in October 1943:

. . . we must be honest, decent, loyal and comradely to members of our own blood and to no one else. What happens to the Russians, what happens to the Czechs, is a matter of utter indifference to me. Such good blood of our own kind as there may be among the nations we shall acquire for ourselves, if necessary by taking away the children and bringing them up among us. Whether the other peoples live in comfort or die of hunger interest me only in so far as we need them as slaves. . . . Whether or not 10,000 Russian women collapse from exhaustion while digging a tank ditch interests me only in so far as the tank ditch is completed for Germany. . . . We Germans, who are the only people in the world who have a decent attitude to animals, will also adopt a decent attitude to these human animals, but it is a crime against our own blood to worry about them. . . . Most of you know what it means to see a hundred corpses lying together, five hundred or a thousand. To have stuck it out and at the same time . . . to have remained decent fellows, that is what has made us hard.

Himmler was by now Minister of the Interior and was thus in authority over the courts and civil service as well as the police and security services. At the same time he was head of the "Waffen-SS" (armed SS), a fully militarized branch of the SS with its own

◁**15** Political detainees at Oranienburg, the first concentration camp.

tanks, artillery and other heavy equipment, which in the course of the war was to expand from three to 35 divisions, rivalling the Wehrmacht (the regular armed services) itself.

Convinced of Himmler's unshakable loyalty, Hitler gave him the task of hunting down and torturing everyone who could be linked with the July 1944 plot to assassinate him. Distrustful of the Army High Command on account of the involvement of senior officers in the assassination plot, the Führer also made Himmler Commander-in-Chief of the Reserve Army and the Volkssturm (Home Guard). In spite of his total lack of military experience Himmler was also put in charge of the defence of Alsace, which he swiftly lost to the advancing Americans.

In his public pronouncements Himmler continued to demonstrate his unswerving devotion to the Nazi cause. His order of the day for 10 September stated that:

◁**16** "The fate of a few filthy, lousy Jews and epileptics is not worth bothering about." Adolf Hitler, 1942.

Every deserter will find his just punishment. Furthermore, his behaviour will entail the most severe consequences for his family. They will be shot.

At the same time, convinced that the war was lost, Himmler began to make his own plans. Through the head of the Swedish Red Cross, Count Folke Bernadotte, he tried to approach the Allies with a view to negotiating peace terms. He proposed to order the surrender of Germany's armies in the west while continuing to fight the Russians in the east, himself taking Hitler's place as leader of Germany. (These terms were about as acceptable to the Allies as they would have been to Hitler had he known about them.) In November 1944, on his own initiative, Himmler forbade the further gassing of Jews and ordered the destruction of the extermination camps. Not until shortly before his own death did Hitler learn, to his utter astonishment, of Himmler's betrayal. Enraged, he stripped him of all his offices and ordered his death. The Reichsführer SS evaded retribution by assuming a false identity, only to be captured by British troops. On 23 May 1945 he committed suicide by swallowing a concealed cyanide capsule.

Reinhard Heydrich (1904-42)

Reinhard Heydrich was to many Nazis the ideal model of the Aryan "superman". Tall, blond and athletic, he was a first-class fencer, horseman and pilot and violinist of concert standard. But he was also a bad sportsman and a cheat, universally unpopular with his fellow officers and tortured by fears that he was himself part Jewish.

Having served as a member of a Freikorps while still only 15 years old, Heydrich entered the navy in 1922 and specialized in intelligence work. In 1931 he was forced to resign after an

honour court found him guilty of "conduct unbecoming to an officer and a gentleman" in an affair involving the daughter of the director of a naval dockyard. Joining the Nazi party in July of the same year, he moved into the SS, attracting Himmler's attention by his energy and arrogant manner. Within a year he had been promoted to Colonel and head of the SD (the SS's own secret police). As a reward for his services during the "Night of the Long Knives" (30 June 1934), he was promoted to SS Lieutenant General. By 1936 he was

17 "That a man as irreplaceable as Heydrich should expose himself to unnecessary danger I can only condemn as stupid and idiotic." Adolf Hitler 1942.

Himmler's right-hand man and effectively in charge of the entire secret police apparatus of the Reich. In 1938 Hitler entrusted him with supervising police activities in Austria after the "Anschluss" (the Nazi takeover).

An expert in "dirty tricks", Heydrich arranged the fake evidence of homosexual activities which led to the disgrace in 1938 of General von Fritsch, who had tried to oppose Hitler's personal takeover of the German armed forces. On 31 August 1939 a German broadcasting station at Gleiwitz (Gliwice) in Silesia, some 10 kilometres from the border

18 "Though all the centuries, force and power are the determining factors. Only force rules. Force is the first law." Adolf Hitler 22 November, 1936.

19 The razing of the village of Lidice.

with Poland, was apparently attacked by a dozen men in Polish uniforms, all of whom were shot dead. Foreign journalists were shown the bodies and reported to the world's press news of this latest Polish "provocation". The next day, Hitler invaded Poland. The attackers were, in fact, prisoners from German concentration camps.

Heydrich's next major tasks were to organize the concentration of Jews from Germany, Austria and Poland into ghettoes and to co-ordinate the activities of the specially recruited "Einsatzgruppen" (action groups), who followed the advancing German armies into Russia, murdering Poles, Jews and Soviet officials in the conquered areas. In September 1941 Heydrich took up a new position as Reich Protector of Bohemia and Moravia. Introducing carrot-and-stick policies to break local opposition to the German occupation, he improved local wages and working conditions and food supplies, while at the same time ordering the mass execution of opponents of the new regime. Confident of his own success in pacifying the Czechs, he dispensed with tight security precautions.

On the morning of 27 May 1942 Heydrich was being driven to his office when his car was attacked with a sub-machine gun and a bomb by two Free Czech agents, trained in England. The assassins fled but were soon caught and massacred on the spot with many other resistance fighters. Heydrich, despite the attentions of one of Hitler's personal physicians, died on 4 June. Both Hitler and Himmler attended his funeral in person and delivered speeches in his praise. Reprisal for his death was swift and terrible. The German occupation forces picked out the village of Lidice, razed it to the ground, shot all the adult male inhabitants and put the women and children in concentration camps. Special courts in Prague and Brno condemned another thousand people to death. In death as in life, Heydrich's name was synonymous with terror.

Albert Speer (1905-81)

As a young man Hitler had twice been refused admission to art school on grounds of "insufficient talent". He remained a frustrated artist all his life. And he saw in the young and talented Albert Speer the man who could turn into reality his grand schemes for rebuilding Europe once it had all come under Nazi rule. But Speer's great abilities were to

20 Architect of defeat? – Speer inspecting coastal fortifications 1944.

be directed mainly to the task of destroying Europe rather than rebuilding it.

The son of an architect and a trained architect himself, Speer first heard Hitler speak in 1930, while he was still a student at university. He was hypnotized. Like many others, he was less convinced by the political ideas that Hitler was putting forward than enthralled by the power of the man's personality. In 1931 he became a party member. The following year he came to Hitler's personal attention when he re-designed the local Nazi party headquarters in Berlin. From 1933 onwards he was made responsible for designing major Nazis parades and rallies, with their striking sequences of

21 Nuremberg Party Rally. Sir Nevil Henderson, the ▷ British Ambassador in Berlin, likened the lighting effects to "a cathedral of ice".

22 Speer's design for a new Chancellery building.

flags, banners, lighting-effects and columns of marching men. His greatest theatrical triumph came at the party rally at Nuremberg in 1936. Speer had been wondering how to distract the crowd's attention from the bloated bodies of the Nazi leaders, fattened by their enjoyment of the fruits of office. Bursting out of their close-cut uniforms they looked like caricatures of Aryan supermen. Speer's solution was simple, ingenious and dramatic – make the onlookers look elsewhere. At a crucial moment in the proceedings massive search-lights were switched on to illuminate the night sky and form a dazzling dome above the massed ranks of the party leaders, suggesting a group of demi-gods suddenly descended from the heavens.

Commissioned to draw up plans for a new Berlin with ten million inhabitants, Speer was also given more specific tasks and loaded with honours. In 1937 his design for the Nuremberg Congress stadium won the Grand Prix at the Paris World's Fair, a major international exhibition of arts and industry. In the same year Hitler gave him the splendid, if rather meaningless, title of Inspector General of the Reich. In 1938 Speer, already an honorary professor, was awarded the Nazi party Golden Badge of Honour. In 1939 he supervised the completion of Hitler's new Chancellery building. (The Russians pounded it to rubble when they took Berlin.) A member of the Reichstag from 1941, Speer was also Inspector of Water and Energy, head of the Nazi party's main office for technology and a member of the Central Planning Office.

Hitler regarded Speer not only as "an architect of genius" but also as a superb organizer with immense administrative abilities. When, therefore, Fritz Todt, the Minister of Armaments and War Production was killed in a plane crash in 1942, Speer, to his amazement, found himself appointed as his successor. The massive increase in output he swiftly achieved led to his being placed in charge of all war production the following year. The transformation of Germany's war economy which Speer effected enabled the Third Reich, as he was later to claim, to fight for another two years, despite military reverses on all fronts and continuous Allied bombing raids by day and night. In 1940, under Goering, fighter production per month was less than 400; in 1944, under Speer, it passed the 3000 mark. In 1941, 2900 heavy tanks were produced; in 1944, 17,300.

Speer's "economic miracle" was brought about by taking production as far as possible out of the hands of agencies controlled by party hacks and state bureaucrats and putting it under the control of a network of committees staffed by some 6000 selected businessmen and technicians. At the same time Speer made a determined attempt to do away with the power of the "Gauleiters" who tried to keep resources and skilled men in their own areas, regardless of needs elsewhere. He also did his best to root out corruption, forbidding the acceptance of such bribes as cameras and radios from firms tendering for contracts. The directive which contained this order also carried a vague and chilling warning:

I cannot protect any of my colleagues who contravene this order, however great their services have been.

Speer's economic success was not, however, entirely the result of brilliant management. It also rested on an enormous expansion of the system of slave labour which had begun under his predecessor.

Uniquely placed to judge the point at which it had become impossible for Germany to win the war, Speer by 1944 had rejected Hitler's policy of "victory or annihilation" and had begun to consider how Germany could be saved from total destruction. He worked on a plan to assassinate Hitler by pumping gas into the bunker beneath the Chancellery, to which Hitler had retreated, but he abandoned this idea as impracticable. He came to despair of overthrowing Hitler when he recognized the depth of loyalty that the Führer still inspired as Germany lurched towards defeat and total ruin. Crouching unrecognized in a bunker near the front line in February 1945, he overheard men talking and realized that:

they believed in Hitler as in no one else, believed that he and only he both understood the working

class from which he had risen and the mystery of politics which had been concealed from the German race – only he could work the miracle of their salvation.

Speer tried to face Hitler with the truth of Germany's hopeless position and, when he failed, tried to resign. Hitler refused to accept his resignation. When Hitler gave the order in the last weeks of the war for the Germans to destroy everything in the face of the advancing Allies, Speer successfully countermanded the Führer's command. And Hitler, who had ordered the arrest of his oldest comarades like Goering and Himmler, did nothing – a tribute to his lasting affection for a "fellow artist".

Fleeing Berlin, Speer was eventually arrested by the British. In marked contrast to

23 In the dock – Speer's final speech before the International Military Tribunal at Nuremburg.

other Nazi leaders, Speer acknowledged his guilt before the International Military Tribunal at Nuremberg, admitting that it was not enough to claim to be "following orders" to escape from responsibility for wicked acts. Although found guilty of war crimes against humanity, Speer was spared the death sentence (against the wishes of the Russians) on the grounds that:

. . . in the closing stages of the war he was one of the few men who had the courage to tell Hitler that the war was lost and to take steps to prevent senseless destruction.

Sentenced at Nuremberg to 20 years' imprisonment for his exploitation of slave labour, Speer used his time in Spandau gaol to draft his memoirs. *Inside the Third Reich* and *The Slave State* remain unique as the only thorough and reliable personal accounts of the Hitler regime by a former Nazi leader of the first rank. Speer was released in 1966, and died on a visit to England in 1981.

In his final speech before his accusers at Nuremberg Speer tried to make some sense of what had happend to him and Germany:

Hitler's dictatorship was the first . . . which employed to perfection the instruments of technology to dominate its own people. . . . Telephone, teletype and radio made it possible to transmit the commands of the highest levels directly to the lowest organs where, because of their high authority, they were executed uncritically. . . . The instruments of technology made it possible to maintain a close watch over all citizens and to keep criminal apparatus shrouded in a high degree of secrecy. To the outsider this state apparatus may look like the seemingly wild tangle of cables in a telephone exchange; but like such an exchange it could be directed by a single will. Dictatorships of the past needed assistants of high quality in the lower ranks of the leadership also – men who could think and act independently. The authoritarian system in the age of technology can do without such men.

Speer's point is certainly a perceptive one; but the suggestion that Nazism can be explained as the outcome of Hitler plus technology will still seem to many to be an inadequate account of what happened in Germany between its defeat in 1918 and its destruction in 1945.

Robert Ley (1890-1945)

The existence of an independent, organized labour movement was one of the most important obstacles to total Nazi domination of Germany's economic and social life. Ironically, the German Labour movement was to be reorganized under the direction of one of the least organized of all the Nazi leaders, Robert Ley, an incompetent administrator and drunkard.

Trained as a chemist, Ley served as an airman in the Great War and was shot down and taken prisoner by the French. When he returned to Germany he went to work for the giant I.G. Farben chemical company until he was dismissed for habitual drunkenness. Joining the Nazi party in 1924, he soon became a close personal associate of Hitler and was rewarded with the appointment of "Gauleiter" of his native Rhineland in recognition of his accomplishments as a street-fighter, gutter journalist and blackmailer of Jews.

Uncouth and in many ways a buffoon, Ley nevertheless won considerable personal popularity for his vitriolic attacks on the wealthy and privileged classes of the old

regime. Regarded as a man gifted with the common touch, he was placed in charge of labour activities in May 1933. With the assistance of the SA and the Gestapo he was soon able to pick off trade union leaders who were inclined to resist being "co-ordinated" by the new government. The outcome was the dissolution of all formerly free and independent unions into a single organization – the "Deutsche Arbeitsfront" (German Labour Front or DAF). With 25 million members it was the largest single organization in Nazi Germany and the largest body of its kind in the modern history of Europe.

The DAF philosophy was based on a denial of class struggle and of the notion of class interests which were opposed to or even distinguishable from those of the nation as a whole. It preached "social peace" and banned strikes. Through a massive network of officials it controlled the hiring and firing of

25 A German Labour Front poster proclaims the ▷ solidarity of management and workers, recalling the comradeship of the trenches. "Then, as now, we remain comrades."

26 Party faithful: the Women's Labour Service.

damals wie heute

Wir bleiben
kameraden

Die Deutsche Arbeits Front

workers, their wage rates and industrial training, social security payments and care for the elderly and disabled. Regimentation by means of uniforms, mass drills and the mouthing of slogans was promoted throughout industry. "Every worker must regard himself as a soldier of the economy", Ley told workers at the Siemens electrical factory in October 1933. A "Beauty of Labour" unit (headed by Albert Speer, Hitler's favourite architect) was established to improve the working environment in plants and factories.

There was regimented work but there was also regimented leisure through the DAF-sponsored "Kraft durch Freude" ("strength through joy") organization which arranged

28 Ley, flanked by Hitler and Dr Porsche, the designer of the Volkswagen.

holiday camps, vacation trips, sports events and cultural activities at heavily subsidized prices. For the first time, many workers were able to attend concerts or the opera, to travel abroad or to make up for lost opportunities in education; in other words, to taste the pleasures of the privileged. And many, no doubt, did see this as an example of socialism in practice.

Meanwhile the DAF empire expanded to embrace hotels, ocean liners, banks, insurance companies, publishing houses and, from 1938, the Volkswagen company, created to mass-produce a "people's car". Money for this scheme was raised by advance payments from workers for cars still to be produced. Some were made, either for export or for propaganda purposes, but none went to the ordinary Germans who had parted with their cash. And a good deal of that cash found its way into the pockets of Robert Ley. Most ordinary workers lost out in other ways as well. Their wages were, in effect, controlled – and declined in real terms. And they were obliged to pay out to large numbers of Nazi "charities" whose activities and expenditures were quite outside their control. They also had considerable difficulty in moving from one job to another.

The sheer scale of the DAF involved Ley in a bewildering variety of tasks, and during the war even more jobs were given to him, including that of supervising the nation's housing programme. He was also given the task of building and organizing the so-called Ordensburg schools – castle-like institutions where the brightest and toughest graduates of special Adolf Hitler schools were to be trained and indoctrinated as the ruling elite of the "New Order" by means of "four years of the hardest possible physical and mental exertions". Ley also played a major part in organizing the recruitment of factory workers and agricultural labourers from German-occupied territories, at first on a voluntary basis and later by force. When the war ended he was in command of the Adolf Hitler corps of volunteer soldiers which had been hastily scratched together for the last-ditch defence of Germany. Arrested by the Allies, he hanged himself in his cell at Nuremberg before being brought to trial. He left behind a letter in which he recommended the reconciliation of Germans and Jews.

Erwin Rommel (1891-1944)

Erwin Rommel was a legend in his own lifetime. Whether or not he should have been is another matter. Certainly, no other German general became more renowned among the British, Nazi Germany's most persistent enemy. Even they gave him a grudging respect as a brilliant tactician and inspiring commander. But Rommel was a soldier's general rather than a general's general. Nazi Germany's greatest military challenge was the Russian front, where generals were required to co-ordinate the movements of dozens of army divisions. Rommel's victories were largely won in North Africa, a side-show, albeit a spectacular one, where he usually commanded two or three divisions and was able to keep in close personal touch with his junior commanders. But the imagination of soldiers and civilians alike applauds skill rather than scale. The Allies acknowledged a worthy opponent in "the Desert Fox"; Hitler chose him as a possible head of state in the event of his own death; troops on both sides spoke of him as a warrior whose chivalry matched his daring. In other words, he was not associated with any atrocities. Indeed, he protested against them. That such behaviour should seem remarkable is itself a comment on the standards of conduct of Nazi Germany's fighting forces. Rommel's protests were private rather than public – not that there was any free press through which to make a public protest – and they were ignored. He was far too popular and too competent to be set aside lightly.

The son of a South German schoolmaster, Erwin Rommel became a career soldier in 1910 and served with distinction in the Great War on the Western Front, in Rumania and in Italy, winning the "Pour le Mérite", Germany's highest decoration for valour. Between the wars Rommel served as the commandant of a garrison of Germany's shrunken army and lectured at various military academies. As the author of a textbook on infantry tactics he attracted the attention of Hitler, who made him commander of his personal bodyguard, although he never actually joined the Nazi party. In 1940 Rommel, as an officer favoured by Hitler, received, at his own request, command of the Seventh Panzer Division. Switching from infantry to tanks without apparent effort, he played a prominent part in the conquest of France. As usual, he showed his ability to gamble, to break the rules and come out the winner. For the loss of 42 tanks and a total of 3000 casualties, he captured 430 armoured vehicles, plus 300 guns and 100,000 prisoners.

In February 1941 Rommel was given command of the Afrika Korps. Within two weeks he had driven the British out of all the territory they had captured in the previous two months. In June 1942 he took the major British stronghold of Tobruk, with large quantities of arms and stores. Promoted Field-Marshal, he was, however, never given enough men and supplies to enable him to win a decisive victory. As he noted in his diary:

Hitler has made me a field-marshal. I would much rather he had given me one more division.

30 Keeping a lookout: the Afrika Korps in the desert. ▷

29 "The name of Field Marshal Rommel will be for ever linked with the heroic battle in North Africa." Adolf Hitler 14 October, 1944.

Rommel excelled in the field, leading, quite literally, from the front. One of his staff officers confessed that:

. . . he was not an easy man to serve; he spared those around him as little as he spared himself.

31   A sentry patrols the Atlantic Wall.

But the same officer conceded that:

Between Rommel and his troops was that mutual understanding which cannot be explained and analysed but which is the gift of the gods. The Afrika Korps followed Rommel wherever he led, however hard he drove them . . . the men knew that Rommel was the last man to spare Rommel.

Hitler, too, had the highest regard for this lucky general. He was, after all, ideally qualified to be a Nazi hero – not upper-class, not Prussian, not on the General Staff and not subtle enough to be a political nuisance. Even the cynical Goebbels recorded in his diary that:

. . . he is such an exemplary character and outstanding soldier that propaganda on his behalf can do no harm. For once propaganda is being done for the right person.

The British military historian Sir Basil Liddell Hart has confirmed this view:

Exasperating to staff officers, he was worshipped by his fighting troops and what he got out of them in performance was far beyond any rational calculation.

Faced with the determined and well-supplied Montgomery, Rommel conducted a skilful fighting retreat from the borders of Egypt back to Tunisia through the winter of 1942-3 until he was finally withdrawn from desert command in March 1943 on account of the strain on his health.

After marking time in northern Italy for some months, Rommel was appointed

32 Death before dishonour? – Rommel's state funeral.

Inspector for Coastal Defences in France, in anticipation of the expected Allied invasion. Finding terrible gaps in the German defences, he worked tirelessly to strengthen the "Atlantic Wall", obsessed with the need to halt the invaders on the beaches. But all his efforts were in vain. When the Allied invasion came on 6 June 1944, Rommel himself was absent on leave, the local commanders were hopelessly at odds with each other and command of the vital mobile reserve was dependent on the direct orders of the Führer – who was asleep.

Rommel did what he could to save the situation but was utterly disillusioned by the scale of the disaster:

It was a terrible blood-letting. Sometimes we had as many casualties in one day as during the whole of the summer fighting in Africa in 1942. My nerves are pretty good but sometimes I was near collapse. It was casualty reports, casualty reports, casualty reports, wherever you went. I have never fought with such losses.

Hitler remained deaf to Rommel's pleas to end the war. Rommel, therefore, let it be known to a number of conspirators among the military that he thought Hitler ought to be arrested and put on trial. He did not, however, become personally involved in the plot to assassinate Hitler, although the plotters intended to make him head of state in the Führer's place.

On 17 July Rommel's staff-car was machine-gunned by a British fighter and he was severely wounded in the head. Three days later Colonel von Stauffenberg (see p. 40) attempted unsuccessfully to blow up Hitler. Rommel's indirect involvement was enough to condemn him to the Führer's vengeance. His prestige, however, was so great than an open scandal was avoided. On 14 October two generals visited him and offered him the choice of suicide by poison or the torture, public trial and execution not only of himself but of his family and personal staff as well. Rommel chose poison. He was buried with full military honours and it was announced that he had died from his wounds.

Leni Riefenstahl (1902-   )

Leni Riefenstahl was the most brilliant film-maker to put her talents at the service of the Nazis. Born in Berlin in 1902, she trained as a ballet dancer before appearing as a film actress for the first time in 1925. After starring in several musical and romantic movies, she established her reputation as a film-maker in her own right with *Das Blaue Licht* (*The Blue Light*) (1932) which she co-authored, directed and produced and in which she also played the leading part. The film was awarded a gold medal at the Venice Biennale Festival of Fine Arts and won Hitler's own personal admiration for her work. As a result, she was invited to make films for the Nazi party, much

33 Leni Riefenstahl.

to the annoyance of Goebbels, who, as Minister of Public Enlightenment and Propaganda, had his own pet film-makers and resented Hitler's favour being shown to any artist outside his own personal control.

Athletic and attractive, Leni Riefenstahl was well-fitted by temperament and talent to translate on to the cinema screen such central themes of Nazi propaganda as the cult of physical toughness, the beauty of the German fatherland and the intoxicating power of mass rallies. Her first production, *Sieg des Glaubens* (*Victory of Faith*) (1933), was a short chronicle of the Nuremberg party rally. *Reichsparteitag* (*Reich Party Day*) (1935) was a full-length film celebration of the Nazi party and its leader.

34 Poster for 1936 Berlin Olympics.

35 Opening ceremony of the eleventh Olympiad. Competitors march past Hitler.

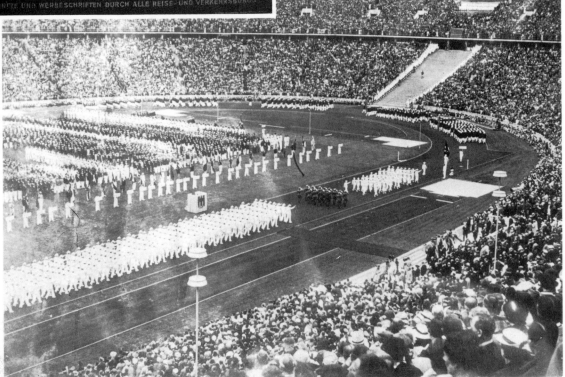

36 Hitler takes his seat at the première of *Triumph of the Will.*

37 A still from *Triumph of the Will.*

Triumph des Willens (*Triumph of the Will* – the title was Hitler's personal suggestion) was produced in the same year and conjured up the heady atmosphere of the 200,000-strong 1934 Nuremberg party rally, the largest in the history of the Nazi movement. With a crew of more than 100 technicians, including 16 cameramen controlling 36 cameras and dozens of spotlights, Leni Riefenstahl combined images of swirling movement, crashing sound and stunning lighting effects to produce an impact worthy of a Wagner opera. The film won a gold prize at the first Venice Film Festival.

The climax of Leni Riefenstahl's career came, however, with her next film, *Olympia* – a four-hour epic, released in two parts and based on the 1936 Olympic Games, which were staged in Berlin. Hitler gave the film his personal seal of approval by attending its gala première on 20 April 1938, his forty-ninth birthday. The Venice Biennale awarded the film its coveted first prize. Even after the war, in 1948, when the Games were held in London, the film was honoured by the International Olympic Committee (although Germany was not invited to send a team to the Games).

Leni Riefenstahl's international success only served to strengthen Goebbels' resentment and he was so able to frustrate her career that she passed the war years in relative obscurity in Austria, unable to mount any major project. Ironically, after the fall of the Third Reich she was one of the few leading figures in the German film industry to suffer for serving the Nazi cause. Vigorously denying both her personal approval of Nazi policies and rumours of romantic involvement with the Führer, she was eventually able to return to filming. In her later years she devoted herself to photographing African peoples, publishing two books of superb pictures, *The Last of the Nuba* and *The People of Kau*.

RESISTERS AND SURVIVORS

Resistance to the Nazis took many forms, from leafleting to assassination, from major conspiracies to individual acts of defiance. But it was always dangerous and often fatal.

Resistance to Nazism as a movement began almost with its birth and usually took the form of street-fighting, most often led by, and frequently started by, the Communists. (After the Nazi takeover, however, many former Communists changed sides and put on the brown uniform of the SA, where they were known as "Beefsteaks", because they were brown outside but still red inside.) The left wing in general, and the Communists in particular, continued to supply the most consistent opposition even after the Nazi takeover had driven them underground and killed their leaders or driven them into exile, as the experiences of Lore Wolf (see pp. 47-51) clearly show.

Resistance to the Nazis as a government embraced the right wing as well as the left, Catholics as well as Communists. As early as 1931 the Protestant preacher Dietrich Bonhoeffer (see pp. 52-55) denounced Nazism for its extremist nationalism and positive approval of pagan myths and rituals from Germany's pre-Christian past. Many conservatives who approved of the Nazis' strong nationalist line were shocked by the racist Nuremberg Laws of 1935, the 1938 "Crystal Night" pogrom (so-called because the streets were littered with broken glass from the windows of Jewish homes and shops) and by the pressures put upon both the Protestant and Catholic churches to support Nazi policies. In the encyclical *Mit brennender Sorge* Pope Pius XI denounced the Nazis' celebration of the pagan cults of blood, sun and soil and warned that the notion of racial superiority was itself a form of idolatry.

But, while some individuals spoke out against the Nazis, others thought it wiser to protect what freedom they had left rather than risk losing it by confronting the government. And many took the view that their concern should be the fate of Christians, not Jews. So, neither the Catholic bishops as a body nor any of the major Protestant sects formally condemned the Nuremberg laws. Equally,

Ein feierlicher Augenblick von der Grundsteinlegung zum Haus der deutschen Kunst.

Der päpstliche Nuntius Basallo di Torregrossa spricht eben zum Führer:

„Ich habe Sie lange nicht verstanden.
Ich habe mich aber lange darum bemüht.
Heute versteh' ich Sie."

Auch jeder deutsche Katholik versteht heute Adolf Hitler und stimmt am 12. November mit:

38 "For a long time I didn't understand you. But I have been trying to. And today I do." Nazi propagandists publicized the Papal Nuncio's ambiguous tribute to Hitler in order to secure Catholic support.

39 "The Nazis are our Calamity".

And thousands actually were in prison. Between 1933 and 1939 the regular courts sentenced 225,000 people to a total of 600,000 years' imprisonment for political offences. These figures do not include – for the figure is not accurately known – the numbers thrown into concentration camps or killed without trial by the police or SA. In April 1939 the Gestapo claimed to be holding in "protective custody" 162,734 prisoners. Over the course of the entire Nazi period (1933-45) at least 800,000 people were condemned to periods of detention for acts of resistance. Moral considerations, as well as fear, inhibited

40 "The old election slogan in the 'new' Reich! Blood and Iron". A warning reference to the similarity between Nazi policies and those of Bismarck who unified Germany by force.

Hitler, for his part, was careful to avoid a direct assault on the Catholic Church as such and restrained those like Goebbels and Bormann who favoured such a course.

Opposition amongst the military was initally held back by the reluctance of professional officers to break the oath of allegiance they had sworn to Hitler as head of state, by the contrived disgrace of Generals Beck and von Fritsch in 1938 and by Hitler's continual foreign policy successes and military victories. Only after 1941, when the war situation began to go against Germany, did serious efforts to mount a coup against Hitler revive. No fewer than five attempts were made to assassinate him. The retribution which followed von Stauffenberg's attempt (see p. 41) showed the price to be paid for failure.

Resistance was constantly frustrated by the immense and ruthless system of policing and surveillance created to perpetuate Nazi rule, which embraced not only the Gestapo and SD, but also thousands of spies and informers. As the socialist Wilhelm Leuschner wrote to a friend in England:

We are locked into an enormous prison and successful rebellion is just as impossible here as against armed guards in any penitentiary [prison].

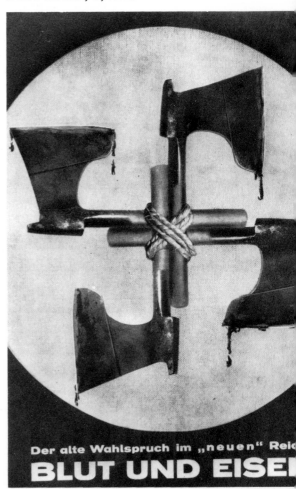

Der alte Wahlspruch im „neuen" Rei

BLUT UND EISE

many. As Count Helmut von Moltke reminded an English friend: for an opponent of Hitler and supporter of democracy in a Nazi-occupied country "moral and national loyalties coincide: for us at home [in Germany] those loyalties are obviously contradictory". But many thousands of Germans overcame this contradiction and in doing so laid the moral foundations of post-war German democracy.

Claus von Stauffenberg (1907-44)

Von Stauffenberg was the man who failed to kill Hitler. A Catholic, an intellectual, a sportsman and a patriot, he was a war hero who tried to end the war.

Claus Schenk, Graf (Count) von Stauffenberg, was born in 1907 in Greifenstein Castle and was a descendent, from both sides of his family, of aristocrats and generals. His father was a high official at the court of the King of Württemberg and the young boy grew up in a family which was both highly cultured and devoutly Christian. In 1926 von Stauffenberg became an officer cadet in the famous Bamberger Reiter, the Seventh Bamberg Cavalry Regiment. Picked out as a man of oustanding promise, he was posted to the War Academy in Berlin in 1936 and promoted to the General Staff two years later. Able and ambitious, he also proved himself to be argumentative. This might have held him back from further promotion in peace-time but the outbreak of war opened up many new opportunities for officers with brains and initiative. Having served with distinction with the Sixteenth Panzer Division in the Polish and French campaigns, von Stauffenberg was transferred to the Army High Command in June 1940.

Von Stauffenberg had, not surprisingly, been brought up as a monarchist and, like many members of Germany's old ruling class, longed passionately for the rebirth of his country's former grandeur. He was not, at first, opposed to the Nazi movement, though he regarded its leaders, including Hitler, with distaste. His conversion to the cause of active resistance came during the invasion of Russia, when he could no longer ignore the barbarities of the SS and the mass slaughter of Jews, Russian civilians and prisoners of war.

41 Von Stauffenberg, aged 27.

In February 1943, von Stauffenberg was posted to Tunisia as Operations Officer of the Tenth Panzer Division. On 7 April he walked into a minefield and was severely wounded, losing his left eye, his right hand and forearm, half his left hand and part of one leg. Thanks to the skill of Doctor Ferdinand Sauerbruch, Hitler's personal surgeon, the sight of von Stauffenberg's right eye was saved. He was, after months of convalescence, able to take up a post in Berlin on the staff of the Deputy Commander of the Reserve Army, General Olbricht, who was already making detailed plans to assassinate Hitler and had set up a government of generals who would smash the Gestapo and the SS and negotiate a compromise peace with the Allies.

In June 1944 von Stauffenberg was made Chief of Staff to General Fromm, the Commander of the Reserve Army. This gave him an official reason to attend military conferences at Hitler's personal headquarters at Rastenburg in East Prussia. As a severely handicapped war hero, von Stauffenberg would be spared the normal body searches. He was, therefore, the ideal person to carry in a time-bomb.

On three occasions von Stauffenberg put a

42 "Wolfsschanze", (the wolf's lair). Hitler's headquarters in East-Prussia.

bomb into his briefcase and smuggled it into those meetings. On the first two occasions – 2 July and 15 July 1944 – he decided not to detonate the bomb because Himmler and Goering were absent. On the third occasion – 20 July 1944 – he decided to go ahead regardless. The Gestapo were searching for one of his fellow conspirators and, if the Allies were to win a decisive victory in Normandy, the plan would be overtaken by events.

Arriving at Rastenburg, von Stauffenberg arranged for his plane to be prepared for an immediate return flight to Berlin. Before entering Hitler's conference room, he stopped off in another building to arm the bomb. He gave himself a margin of ten minutes. It took three precious minutes to pass the various guards around the conference room. When he arrived he was greeted personally by Hitler. He apologised for being slightly late and tried to stay as close to the Führer as possible. Having placed the briefcase under the map-table around which Hitler and his generals were standing, von Stauffenberg excused himself to take an urgent pre-arranged telephone call. By the time the bomb went off he was already in his car and minutes later was coolly bluffing his way out of the Führer's headquarters.

Half an hour after the explosion, von Stauffenberg was on his way back to Berlin. When he arrived, more than two hours later, he found that nothing had been done to seize power in the capital, although several generals had taken over in various provincial cities and in Paris.

What he did not know at the time was that Hitler had not been killed. Von Stauffenberg's briefcase had been moved to the far end of the map-table, away from the Führer. And the full force of the explosion had been lost, because, it being a warm summer's day, all the buildings' windows had been left wide open. Four officers had been killed when the bomb went off and seven more seriously wounded, but Hitler himself suffered only sprains, burns and a shattered eardrum. However, still thinking they had succeeded in killing the

Führer, von Stauffenberg and his fellow conspirators belatedly set about taking over the government in Berlin. The attempted coup was soon crushed by definite news of Hitler's survival and by Goebbels' skill in winning over the officer sent to arrest him.

Von Stauffenberg, together with Olbricht and two other fellow-conspirators, were seized in the War Ministry. Wounded in the scuffle leading to his arrest, he did not suffer long but, in the full glare of car headlights, was machine-gunned to death alongside his comrades in the courtyard of the building. His last words were: "Long live our sacred Germany". The bodies were buried the same night. Later, Himmler sent men to dig them up, burn them and scatter their ashes to the winds.

Over the next months some 7000 other people alleged to have been connected with the conspiracy were executed.

43 After the blast.

Peter Schwiefert (1917-45)

On 15 January 1939 a good-looking, shabbily-dressed young man went to the office of the German Consul in Lisbon, Portugal, and made a formal declaration that he wished "to be regarded henceforth as a Jew and to be subject to all the laws concerning Jews". He knew quite well what this meant, as he explained in a letter to his father:

If this declaration is considered valid in Berlin the letter 'J' will be inscribed on my passport and I shall be given the first name Israel. . . . I shall become an emigrant in perpetuity and shall never be able to return to Germany. (Peter Schwiefert, *The Bird Has No Wings*, Search Press Ltd.)

The young man's name was Peter Schwiefert and he was just 22 years old.

Peter Schwiefert's father was a successful German playwright. Peter's mother, whom he adored, was beautiful, witty and a Jewess. Having divorced Peter's father and then a second husband, she had married into a wealthy Prussian family with extensive business and political connections with the Nazis. Her position of privilege, and her indifference to Judaism as a religion, gave her a sense of security which her son did not share. His decision to go into exile in Portugal in October 1938 had infuriated her as the theatrical gesture of a boy who was as impetuous as he was impractical.

This impression must certainly have been confirmed by Peter's early letters from the fishing village of Faro, where he first settled:

You know I've not learned any skills, so you can understand how limited my possibilities are – at best, and this would need a miracle, they would only keep my head above water.

Even his decision to acknowledge his Jewish heritage seemed almost as much a matter of perversity as of principles:

It is not a religious conversion. I know nothing about the Christian religion or the Jewish religion. But Judaism as such is the only form of Jewish life and there's no other possible way of bearing witness to it. . . . I've had to smile more than once at the strange way Jews have reacted to my decision. They all implore me to go back on it. But always for practical reasons.

Practical reasons evidently had little influence on Peter Schwiefert, but this was not the case with his mother. Even as Peter was announcing his conversion to Judaism, she

44 Peter Schwiefert in Free French army uniform.

was giving up Protestantism to become a fervent convert to the Russian Orthodox Church. After the pogroms of the "Crystal Night" of 9-10 November 1938 she had suddenly realized the extreme danger of her position. Her husband, hard-pressed by his family, who had always disapproved of his marriage to a Jewess, arranged for a speedy divorce and paid a Bulgarian business friend to marry her. By thus acquiring the nationality of a power friendly to Nazi Germany Peter's mother became free to flee the country with her two young daughters – who still did not even know that they were Jewish.

When at last he learned what had happened Peter was horrified:

. . . it can't be, and isn't a matter of belief – with you any more than with me. . . . It's no longer a matter of Judaism or Christianity but solely of 'Hep-Hep' [the shout by Nazis chasing Jews in the street] . . . this is not aimed at the Jewish *religion* . . . but at the Jew as such. The order is: Beat the Jew! and he's beaten. . . . He can protest, he can pray, he can be clever and get away. . . . There's just one thing he can't do. He can't say, I'm not what you think I am . . . whether he loves, hates, accepts, glories in or execrates his Jewishness, whether he has 20 Jewish grand-parents or . . . is a half-Jew, he is always a Jew and it's always a special 'Hep-Hep' that sounds in his ears. . . . I didn't make my decision so as to become a different person. . . . I don't want to shed my skin, like you. I'm not adopting a new religion. I'm not changing course in mid-stream. *I am a Jew and I say so.* . . . With others, everyone knows that they're Jews and they don't need to publish the fact. But with me it isn't known and this is why I have to proclaim it.

Peter Schwiefert did eventually come to accept his mother's new situation and wrote regularly to her at her new home in Bulgaria. As the months passed he was able to report that he had achieved a modest prosperity, progressing from a precarious existence as an occasional teacher of German and English to the position of clerk with a firm of sardine exporters. He admitted that he missed concerts and the theatre. Most of all, he was saddened by his continuing failure to realize his chosen ambition – to become a writer. But he had the sense to know his good fortune compared with that of others and reproached his mother for the frivolous attitude of his young step-sisters:

While your children are having a good time and enjoying life, hundreds of Jews aboard a ship near the South American coast have been refused permission to land by all the countries of that continent and are signing a declaration saying they will commit suicide if they are sent back to Germany. That's what we should be thinking about and nothing else.

In October 1939, a year after leaving Germany, Peter Schwiefert reported happily to his mother:

I have been given my carte d'identité, valid for five years. That means I can now enjoy relative security and not live in constant fear of being expelled.

A month later Salazar, the Portuguese dictator, decided to please Hitler by expelling all German Jews. Peter Schwiefert was arrested and held in prison for over three months. In his letters he took care to keep this from his mother – not knowing that when he was released in March 1940 it was thanks to her efforts and her money that he was able to travel via Barcelona and Rome to a new exile in Athens.

A practised survivor after nearly two years in exile, Peter Schwiefert was at first quite confident of his ability to find work of some sort in Greece. But every effort ended in failure, as did his attempts to emigrate to Brazil or Bolivia. Only money sent by his mother from Bulgaria enabled him to survive long enough to reach another major decision. By August 1940 he was sure that:

. . . it's only England's victory that counts; I hope for it more ardently than for anything else in the world, I can think of nothing else. The victory of civilization over barbarism, the victory of human values and human dignity over the boot, over an

45 Peter's statement.

fought in Syria, Libya, Tunisia, Italy (where he was wounded in the shoulder) and finally in France. In November 1944 he wrote to his mother (who had no idea that he had become a soldier) for the first time in four years:

I'm huddled in a tent in the middle of the woods. I'm cold, it's raining, it's autumn. . . . We're in the front line and opposite us are the Germans. . . . Apart from sporadic gunfire and the thunder of artillery now and again, all is quiet. . . . But the end is near. Germany lies before us, not far off, we'll soon be there. . . . Yes, they will be crushed. . . . And the Nazis will suffer as they have made others suffer, and those who aren't Nazis shall suffer too! For they are all responsible, they are all guilty, except a few, except a tiny minority, who chose exile and the struggle for a just cause, or who were unable to flee but resisted all temptation and kept their hands clean. But the others will pay and pay dear. . . . Also at hand is our liberation, the end of this dog's life, for making war is a dog's life . . . what I want most of all: to enter Berlin! For my satisfaction, for my vengeance, so that they can see that I was right! I don't know whether this will be possible, perhaps not. . . .

Peter Schwiefert never did see his native Berlin again. On 7 January 1945 he was in a trench outside the village of Rossfeld, just over a mile from the Rhine. A shell landed beside him in the trench, killing him instantly – two days after his twenty-eighth birthday. Peter Schwiefert's mother received his last letter almost six months after his death. When the war ended she returned to Germany where she died of multiple sclerosis in 1949.

appalling, sickening, limitless tyranny. It's in England where the fate of the battle will now be decided, that the vanguard of mankind is fighting . . .

In December 1940, having been turned down by a British Army wary of alien volunteers, Peter Schwiefert was enlisted at Athens into the Free French forces under the command of General Charles de Gaulle. Over the course of the succeeding four years he

Walter Krämer (1927-   )

Walter Krämer was born in Marburg, the only son of a Jewish shopkeeper, whose family had lived in Germany for centuries. When Hitler

came to power in 1933 Walter was just six, but even at that age he quickly became aware that Jews were now under open attack:

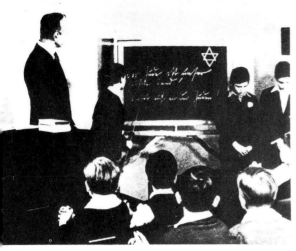

46 Jewish boys being humilitated before their classmates. On the blackboard is written "The Jews are our greatest enemy."

How often my sisters and I would come home from school crying because the teacher had abused us so terribly. I will never forget one of the things he said – "God created the whites and the blacks, too: but the Jew, that mongrel, comes from the devil." Then we didn't understand the words as well as we would today, it was enough to excite the other children so that there was always violence after class. How often I came home bleeding. . . . My parents tried their best, yet they could do little to change this suffering and misery. . . . I still remember the words of our mother "You were born to suffer." (Eugene C. Black and Leonard W. Levy [eds.] *A Documentary History of Western Civilization*, Macmillan Press)

One evening in November 1938 the Krämer family were sitting quietly at home when ten Nazis burst into their house and beat Walter's father unconscious. Later that night every window in the house was smashed. The next day Walter's father was arrested and sent to the concentration camp at Buchenwald. To everyone's joy and relief he was released a week or so later; but the family shop was confiscated, together with any gold or silver things they owned. Walter was ordered to attend a separate school for Jews in Frankfurt. Six months later the Krämers managed to arrange for Walter's eldest sister, Ilse, to go to America. But no one else could leave.

In April 1941 Walter went home to Marburg for his grandfather's funeral. It was the last time he was to see his own father. In December 1941 Walter, along with his mother and youngest sister, Reni, was sent to a camp at Riga, in Latvia. They had been told that Walter's father would join them. He never did. Nor did their luggage. They arrived with only what they could carry. The temperature was minus 45° Centigrade.

Walter was soon set to work in the forests outside the city, digging vast ditches. The work-party was told that the ditches were emplacements for anti-aircraft guns. They soon found out from Russian prisoners that, they were, in fact, mass graves. Walter began to learn the art of survival. He got an indoor job in the camp's shoe-repair shop. Here he was able to steal bits of leather which he traded for scraps of food with Latvians who came into the camp to work. The penalty for bartering was death – by hanging for the person who was caught and by shooting for the rest of his family:

And still it did not stop because living conditions in the camp were so grim that no one could survive without barter. . . . It was death one way or another.

In 1943 Walter was transferred to another camp near Riga, where conditions were even harsher:

We got a cross of oil paint on our backs and chests and a white stripe along the leg of our trousers. Anything extra we wore was stripped off. Our hair was cropped and a cross was cut diagonally on the top of our heads; we later called it the louse track, which it actually was.

Walter was put in a work-group which was commanded by a brutal criminal, and which was building a dam. Every day at least two men died from exhaustion, beating, drowning or execution because they had not been working fast enough. After a month Walter manged to get himself re-assigned by faking illness.

In October 1943 Walter was moved to

another camp where he was set to make shoes for the SS. Here he continued to steal and barter until one day he was caught with a can of tinned fish. He was "let off" with a beating so bad that he was unable to stand or lie down for three days. A week before this incident his best friend, who had also been caught with food and beaten, had hanged himself for fear that the SS would beat him into betraying the names of his accomplices.

When the Russian army advanced to within 20 kilometres of Riga the prisoners in the camps were shipped back to Germany. For a while Walter worked as an electrician in the dockyards at Danzig (now Gdansk in Poland), but when the Russians began to close in on Danzig in turn, Walter and his comrades were force-marched 80 kilometres to a camp at Rieben:

The camp was incredibly overcrowded with prisoners who hadn't eaten for six days. . . . I still had two frozen turnips in my pocket which they tore from my hands. . . . We . . . got a hundred grams of bread for four days, a watered-down soup in the afternoons, and sometimes nothing at all. Nevertheless, we had to work building tank traps. Every day twenty men died. At night we lay on bare cement floors, without blankets, between the dead and the dying. . . . Within four weeks our numbers had dropped from six hundred to thirty . . .

On 11 March 1945 the commandant of the camp received orders to execute all the remaining prisoners at midnight. The Russian army, in the shape of an officer and ten soldiers, arrived an hour before the order was due to be carried out.

The entire camp guard was taken prisoner and met their just punishment before our very eyes, ending up in the mass grave which they had dug for us the day before.

47 Roll-call at Sachsenhausen.

Local German people were brought in to bury the hundreds of prisoners who had died in the weeks before the liberation. The survivors were barely alive. Walter Krämer himself weighed just 30 kilos (under five stone). The Russians did all they could to help:

. . . even though they knew that we had typhoid. They cleaned the barracks, built beds and laid us on straw mattresses. They gave us everything in the way of food and medication that we were able to take. . . . With rice and wheat cereal . . . we were coddled back to health like little children.

48 Survivors at Mauthausen, freed by Soviet troops.

Even then some of the men still died because of fatal internal injuries. . . . Thanks to the Russian care and nursing, we had so far recovered within eight weeks that we could set out for home.

Home. Walter Krämer went home to Marburg. His father had been murdered at Buchenwald. His mother had been gassed at Auschwitz. No one could tell him where his sister was, or even if she was still alive. He was just 18 years old.

Lore Wolf (1900-   )

"Twenty times I was caught, nineteen times I got away." That is the shortest way of telling the story of Lore Wolf, born Eleonore Winkler in 1900 in the village of Summerhausen in Lower Franconia.

Her father was a poor weaver who became a worker in a chemical factory. An accident at the factory left him an invalid for life. As a result of her father's injury Lore's family lived in great poverty. Fourteen years old when the Great War broke out, Lore worked in a munitions factory for 18 months but escaped by learning shorthand and typing at night school. Finding work with the local town council, she came into contact with Social Democrats and then joined a trade union and a youth movement called "Friends of Nature" which organized hikes in the mountains and political discussions.

During the turbulent years following Germany's defeat, Lore took part in many labour demonstrations and marches. In 1923 she protested personally at the arrest of her employer, a Socialist mayor, by the French forces then occupying part of Germany. For a year she went to work in Frankfurt, beyond the reach of the French. Here she met Hans, a young Communist. They were soon married and two years later had a daughter, Hannelore.

By 1928 both Lore and her husband were unemployed. They decided to emigrate to the United States and arrived just in time for the Wall Street Crash and the collapse of the American economy. The sight of terrible hardship in a country famed for its wealth strengthened the Communist beliefs of Lore and her husband. In 1932 they left America for the USSR, where they went to work in a brand-new car factory at Nizhni-Novgorod. As "foreign experts", Lore and her husband had certain privileges with regard to food and living conditions; but that did not prevent Lore and her daughter from catching typhus, although they both recovered safely.

From Germany Lore and her husband heard news of the Nazi takeover. They feared for their relatives, most of whom were Socialists or Communists. Lore persuaded Hans that they should visit Germany to reassure themselves. As soon as they stepped off the train at Frankfurt station their passports and return tickets were confiscated by the Gestapo. Lore's immediate reaction was to join the Communist party – which had just been banned. As a trained typist she was soon producing secret newsletters for Red Aid, the underground Communist resistance organization. Even this was a dangerous business, requiring many precautions:

The necessary paper had to be bought in a number of different shops, as the purchase of larger quantities . . . could have drawn the attention of the Gestapo to our group. . . . The stencils were typed at a different place each time . . . the typing could only be done during the day-time so that it would be lost in the general noise. . . . When [stencils] were finished the typewriter carriage was wiped well, every trace was removed, a few harmless letters were left lying about, then I left the flat with a loud, well-audible 'Heil Hitler' to pass on what I had written. (Lore Wolf, *One Life is Not Enough*, People's Press)

Distribution was another problem:

A leaflet intended for the general public was carried by the wind from walls, houses, viaducts; in large stores it fluttered down from the galleries. In trams passengers found it on their seats, housewives under the door-mats and in their letter-boxes; people out for a walk discovered it . . . on seats and on the ground . . . some of them dared not pick up the leaflet, they read it standing . . . left it lying there and continued on their walk.

These resistance activities went on for 18 months, until Lore's group was betrayed by its leader, whose fiancée had been arrested by the Gestapo. Lore heard how four of her comrades had been picked up by the police, so she hugged her nine-year-old daughter goodbye and fled to the Saar, a region still at that time beyond Nazi control. In her absence her parents were sent to prison for three months to punish her. And her husband was also locked up for his part in the work of Red Aid. In the Saar, Lore devoted himself to helping other political refugees and carrying on propaganda to warn the local people what a Nazi takeover would mean.

When the Nazis did take over in the Saar, Lore fled to Paris, where she demonstrated and worked for the cause of the Republican government of Spain, now plunged into civil war. After a short time she went on to Switzerland where she was briefly reunited with her husband and daughter. Lore continued to organize more illegal resistance activities and Hans, a trained leatherworker, made suitcases with secret compartments for smuggling currency and documents.

But the family was soon split up again when, denounced by Nazi sympathizers, Lore Wolf was expelled by the Swiss authorities for engaging in forbidden political activities which might conflict with Switzerland's neutrality. She slipped back into Switzerland almost immediately and finally returned to France in 1938 and began to organize anti-Nazi propaganda in a frontier area, until the French authorities ordered her to move out. Moving on to Paris, she soon made herself useful as a courier, carrying secret messages between different resistance leaders.

When war broke out in September 1939 many Communist refugees in France were arrested. Lore set herself to knitting socks, which were bought by the French military supplies department. With the money she earned from doing this she bought extra food for her imprisoned friends. Then she went off to the south of France, to work in a munitions factory, using her wages for the same purpose. But even though there was a war on and Lore was making bombs to be dropped on her own country, she never forgot that she was a trade-unionist and organized a successful agitation to get women workers in the factory paid as the same rate as the men.

The collapse of the French army in the summer of 1940 brought Lore back to Paris, where she began to help the newly conquered French to organize their own anti-Nazi resistance. Her own special task was to translate leaflets aimed at the German occupation troops.

On 30 August 1940 Lore Wolf was arrested by the Gestapo. Once again she had been betrayed. After several weeks of

49 Lore Wolf with her daughter, in 1940.

50 "Hitler is the war. Only Hitler's ruin can bring us peace".

HITLER IST DER KRIEG

NUR HITLERS STURZ BRINGT UNS DEN FRIEDEN

interrogation, she was transported back to Germany. Seven years after leaving Frankfurt she had returned to be imprisoned there. On 3 May 1941, almost a year after her arrest, Lore Wolf was at last brought before a Nazi "People's Court" in Berlin. Charged with high treason, she was found guilty and sentenced to 12 years' penal servitude. In January 1944, more than three years after her arrest, Lore was allowed to see her 19-year-old daughter for one hour.

As the war drew to a close, the Allied bombing of Germany intensified and the imprisoned mother feared daily for the life of her child. Soon she had cause to fear for her own:

In front of the prison the SA are burning large bundles of files. . . . The SA men run as if obsessed, poke the pyres, hastily burn documents relating to their atrocities. . . . On 29 March the tension becomes unbearable. All around the prison SS and SA men are posted. The Americans are coming closer and closer. . . . The women can no longer be held back. . . . The prison governor and the matron are helpless. . . . Tumult rages throughout the building. All discipline has ceased.

But the prisoners stopped short of a break-out, fearing the SS would simply shoot them down. Instead, they submitted to being loaded on to cattle-trucks and carried away by rail, two hours before the long-awaited Americans stormed the gaol.

Days later the prison train stopped outside the gates of the concentration camp at Belsen.

In our trucks there are 60 women. . . . We feel indescribably cold. Our dry tongues stick to our gums, our lips are swollen. . . . All of us are ill, diarrhoea, a dreadful stench.

Then they glimpsed three inmates of Belsen, skeletons whose misery exceeded even their

52 Communist resistance sticker: "We must unite against Hitler".

own. For hours they waited, knowing that to enter Belsen was to receive a death sentence. Then, without any explanation, the train pulled away. Days later they finally ended their journey at Hamburg and were taken to a nearby prison camp. Everyone knew that the end of the war was only days away. The women feared that the SS would try to poison them all, and so:

every meal-time before we receive the watery soup . . . we force the chief wardress to taste it first. She is afraid of the future and does not refuse.

Then the British arrived.

I report on our experiences, the frightful suffering, the prison officers who have maltreated us, but also those who have helped us not to lose our trust in human beings.

Three weeks later Lore Wolf was the first German political prisoner to be released from the camp. Reunited with her husband and daughter after so many years of separation, she lived on for many years to become a celebrated member of the West German Communist Party.

◁ 51 Trophies. SA and SS pose with captured Communist banners.

Dietrich Bonhoeffer (1906-45)

I pray for a defeat of my Fatherland. Only through a defeat can we atone for the terrible crimes which we have committed against Europe and the world. (Eberhard Bethge, *Bonhoeffer*, Fount Paperbacks, 1979)

Such was the prayer of Dietrich Bonhoeffer. It was answered less than a month after his death on 9 April 1945 in the concentration camp at Flossenburg.

Dietrich Bonhoeffer was born in Breslau in 1906, the son of a university professor. While still a child he committed himself to the Church and went on to study theology in Tübingen, Berlin and New York. A university lecturer himself at the age of 25, Bonhoeffer was also a trainee pastor in Berlin; he was, therefore, in a good position both to observe the effect of the Nazis coming to power and to publicize his immediate opposition to their anti-Jewish policies and to the concentration of all power in the hands of a single leader.

From 1933 to 1935, however, Bonhoeffer served as pastor of the German Lutheran Church in London. This removed him from the struggle against the Nazis but strengthened his ties with Christians in Britain. These were to be vitally important during the war when he was to join others in seeking a negotiated peace for Germany.

Returning home, Bonhoeffer, though not yet 30, was appointed head of an Evangelical teacher-training college. Alarmed at the way in which the Nazis were trying to take over the Confessional Church by promoting pastors who would not protest at their policies, Bonhoeffer used his position to promote a spirit of resistance to Nazi policies among the new generations of trainee pastors. He also tried, in 1936, to get the Confessional Church to pass a resolution declaring that the "Nuremberg Laws", which made Jews second-class citizens, were a basic violation of their human rights. Bonhoeffer insisted that

53 Dietrich Bonhoeffer.

Christianity could not be reconciled with Nazism and its racist teachings, that churchmen must be free to preach the Gospel without political interference and that Christians had a duty to resist Hitler and to aid victims of Nazi persecution. He declared boldly that: ". . . the church is only a church, when she exists for those outside herself", and that Christians have an "unconditional obligation towards the victims of every social system, even if they do not belong to the Christian community". Bonhoeffer also kept up his contacts with Christian churches abroad, visiting Britain and the United States in 1939.

Teaching, organizing and protesting were methods of resistance. But so too was thinking. And Bonhoeffer was a trained theologian, a man who had chosen to devote himself to trying to understand God and the relationship between God and the world God had created. How should a Christian act in a country which had been taken over by men whose rule was opposed to basic Christian principles of justice, tolerance and compassion? In trying to answer this question Bonhoeffer worked out ways of thinking about God and Christian belief which helped him deal with his own crisis and understand Germany's crisis as well. Bonhoeffer rejected the view that God was some sort of separate, "magical" person "out there", somewhere in the universe. Rather, he suggested, we should think of God as the true essence of all beings who could think and feel and, through thinking and feeling, achieve self-awareness and fulfilment and thus make a reality of God in their lives. God is not, therefore, in Bonhoeffer's view, a remote and mysterious power to whom we can turn for help in our hour of need. We must think of God rather differently, as the source of the strength which lies within us all. God, in other words, is neither to be found nor experienced outside ourselves but rather within us and through our actual living.

In 1940 Bonhoeffer's seminary was closed down for a second time. The Gestapo banned him from preaching or publishing. So, along with his older brother Klaus, an official with the German airline, Lufthansa, and his brother-in-law, Hans von Dohnanyi, Bonhoeffer joined the underground opposition which sought slowly and carefully to build a network of conspirators who could overthrow Hitler and Nazism. Dohnanyi was one of the best-placed to act. Recognized by his superiors as a brilliant young man, he was attached to the Reich Ministry of Justice, where he began to compile a secret dossier documenting in detail the crimes perpetrated by the Nazis under the cover of the law. When war broke out Dohnanyi joined the "Abwehr", the army's intelligence service, where he continued his work of documentation.

In May 1942 it was Bonhoeffer who had the opportunity to help the conspiracy forward by seeking help from the outside. Neutral Sweden provided the meeting-place for Bonhoeffer and Dr George Bell, the Bishop of Chichester and President of the Universal Christian Council for Life and Work. Bell was known for his consistent refusal to identify all German people with the Nazis. (After the war he was to play a leading part in re-establishing links between the German churches and other churches.)

Bonhoeffer told the trusted Bishop Bell:
– that there was a large and active conspiracy against Hitler inside Germany and that the conspirators wanted the Allied governments to be aware of this.
– that the conspirators needed to be assured that the Allies would negotiate peace terms with them if Hitler were overthrown.

54 Hans von Dohnanyi.

55 Bonhoeffer inside Tegel Prison.

– that, as far as the conspirators were concerned, the terms of any settlement would guarantee an end to the persecution of the Jews, withdrawal of all German troops to the frontiers of 1919, a break-up of the alliance with Japan and co-operation with the Allies in the reconstruction of Europe.

Bishop Bell passed Bonhoeffer's message to the British Foreign Secretary, Anthony Eden, but he replied that he saw no good purpose in entering into any agreement with the conspirators. Partly, this reflected suspicion that Germany might seek a "cheap peace", at a time when the Allies were becoming committed to the objective of forcing Germany into accepting an unconditional surrender; partly, it reflected the fear that Germany might seek a separate peace with the Western powers to split them off from Soviet Russia, thus breaking up the Grand Alliance; partly, it reflected doubts about the actual power and willingness of the conspirators to strike. The only thing that could really convince the British government was action, not words.

The failure of his mission did not deter Bonhoeffer from further resistance. In his own words, "Hitler is the Anti-Christ. We must therefore continue with our work and root him out." For Bonhoeffer, resistance was a moral duty – an "act of penitence" – no matter how slight the prospect of success. And the need to combat such total evil necessarily overrode any moral qualms that the resister might have about the deception and violence that were inevitably involved.

Bonhoeffer's active resistance was soon, however, to come to an end. In October 1942 an agent of the "Abwehr" was arrested by the Gestapo and charged with smuggling currency across the German-Swiss border. Unfortunately for the opposition to Hitler, the agent in question revealed under interrogation the names of various members of the "Abwehr" who were engaged in conspiracy – including Dohnanyi. It took six months to follow up the trail thus uncovered by chance. Bonhoeffer, his brother Klaus and von Dohnanyi were all to be arrested and eventually executed.

Dietrich Bonhoeffer was arrested on 5 April

1943 and charged with subverting the armed forces. He spent some 18 months in captivity, awaiting trial. After the failure of the July 1944 plot to assassinate Hitler, Bonhoeffer was transferred to Buchenwald and then to Flossenburg. A fellow-prisoner in Buchenwald paid tribute to the extraordinary radiance of his personality:

. . . he always seemed to be able to diffuse an atmosphere of happiness, of joy in every smallest event in life, and of deep gratitude for the mere fact that he was alive.

Kept in solitary confinement most of the time, Bonhoeffer busied himself writing poems, essays and letters, some of which he managed to get smuggled out. They are a moving testimony to one man's strength and goodness in the face of evil and despair.

Martin Niemöller (1892-1984)

Martin Niemöller was a war hero who became a peace hero. A U-boat commander in the Great War, he was later a passionate campaigner against nuclear weapons and a strenuous opponent of the Nazis, although he volunteered to serve in the war they started.

Friedrich Gustav Emil Martin Niemöller was born in Lippstadt, Westphalia in 1892, the son of a Protestant pastor. Entering the German navy as a midshipman in 1910, he volunteered for submarine service in the Great War and was awarded the "Pour le Mérite," Germany's highest decoration for valour, for his exploits. When the war ended, he refused to surrender his ship to the British as ordered.

In the chaos of the post-war period, Niemöller at first joined one of the para-military units formed to oppose Communist revolutionaries. Then, in 1924, following in his father's footsteps, he became a Protestant minister, working initially as secretary in the Evangelical Church's office for social welfare. In 1931 he became pastor of the fashionable Berlin parish of Dahlem, where his reputation as a naval hero and his extraordinary powers as a preacher combined to draw large congregations to his services. His popularity was confirmed in 1934 by the publication of his memoirs, *From U-boat to Pulpit*. Even the Nazi press praised the book for its patriotic sentiments.

56 Niemöller as First World War hero.

Like many patriots and conservatives, Niemöller was appalled by the corruption, selfishness and disorder of the Weimar period, which he referred to as "fourteen years of darkness", but he soon saw that the Nazi drive to "clean up" Germany masked an even greater threat to its future. The introduction of racist laws into the Church itself in July 1933 made the position quite clear to him. By September he had organized the "Pfarrernotbund", (the Pastors' Emergency League), a union of clergymen opposed to the spread of Nazi ideas among Christians. Out of this grew the "Confessing" or "Spiritual" Church, the 7000-strong opposition to the Nazi-sponsored German Christian Movement, which aimed to capture the official institutions of the Protestant churches. In May 1934 a special meeting of the Spiritual Church at Barmen in the Rhineland affirmed that:

We repudiate the fictitious doctrine that the church must preach to its faithful of events, powers, entities and truths other than those vouchsafed to us by the revelation of God.

Hitler himself was sufficiently concerned by these activities to send for Niemöller personally. But the pastor stood firm against the Führer's reproofs and threats. Prohibited from preaching on several occasions, he refused to be silenced permanently. On 19 June 1937 he told his congregation:

Heaven help us if we made a German Gospel out of the Gospel, a German church out of Christ's church, German Christians out of Evangelical Christians.

A week later he was arrested by the Gestapo and charged with making "malicious attacks against the state".

Formally acquitted of serious charges in February 1938, Niemöller was, however, re-arrested on Hitler's personal orders and held for a further seven years, mostly in solitary confinement, in the concentration camps of Sachsenhausen and Dachau. Nevertheless, when the world war broke out in 1939, he volunteered once more to serve in the navy, putting patriotism before prudence. His offer was rejected, much to his later relief. In the course of the war one of his sons was to be killed fighting on the eastern front and his sermons were to be published in England in 1941 under the title *The Gestapo Defied*. Niemöller remained one of Hitler's most celebrated prisoners. His wife told him in one of the few letters that reached him, that "even the Eskimos are praying for you". Shortly before his own death, however, Hitler finally ordered the execution of numerous prominent prisoners, including Niemöller. But the order was either never received or simply ignored. Whichever was the case, Niemöller, by then transferred to Italy, was released by American troops.

When the war ended, Niemöller was determined to do all he could to restore links between the German churches and churches in other countries. Despite his own resistance to the Nazis, he believed it to be an essential first step to confess his own guilt in not opposing them more successfully:

First they came for the Jews. I was silent. I was not a Jew. Then they came for the Communists. I was silent. I was not a Communist. They they came for the trade unionists. I was silent. I was not a trade unionist. Then they came for me. There was no-one left to speak for me.

Niemöller, as President of the Lutheran Evangelical Church's Office for Foreign Relations, took a leading part in organizing the Stuttgart Declaration (1945), which professed the responsibility of Germany for starting the war and of German churchmen for their complicity in it. Three years later the World Council of Churchmen was established in Amsterdam and Niemöller was among the German delegation welcomed into membership. His speaking tours of Britain, America and Australia during the 1950s won him great personal popularity and showed among the victor powers the human and spiritual worth of the defeated.

A patriot still, Niemöller began to see the best way for his divided homeland being the

57 Germany's conscience.

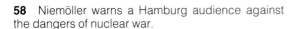

establishment of a reunited but neutral and disarmed Germany. The first step would have to be reconcilation with the East and to this end he made a controversial trip to the Soviet Union in 1952, where he pleaded on behalf of German prisoners-of-war still held in Russian camps. His intercession secured the release of some prisoners. In 1954 he became converted to pacifism and pressed for nuclear disarmament on the ground that "you cannot both love your enemies and threaten to exterminate them". These views were unpopular with many politicians and newspapers. In 1956 Niemöller lost his position as head of the Church's foreign affairs department and in 1959 the West German Defence Minister, Herr Franz Josef Strauss,

58 Niemöller warns a Hamburg audience against the dangers of nuclear war.

tried to have him charged with defaming the armed forces. From 1961 to 1968, however, he served as a senior official of the World Council of Churches. Internationally, his position was unassailable.

Retiring from official German Church duties in 1964, Niemöller continued to travel and preach on behalf of peace and reconcilation. He died in 1984, aged 92, a holder at the same time of the Soviet Union's Lenin Peace Prize and of the highest award of the West German state.

Ilse Koehn (1929-   )

59 Ilse Koehn.

Ilse Koehn was born in 1929, the first child of Grete Dereck, a seamstress, and Ernst Koehn, an electrician with the Berlin Light and Power Company. Both her parents were members of the Social Democratic Party and, from the first, were opponents of the Nazis. Ernst Koehn's mother, whom Ilse knew as Oma ("Granny"), was Jewish by birth, although she never practised her religion. But, after the pronouncement of the "Nuremberg Laws" on 14 November 1935 this ancestry made Ernst Koehn a "Mischling, first degree" because he had two Jewish grandparents. Ilse was therefore a "Mischling, second degree", a person with one Jewish grandparent. Neither were, therefore, "pure Aryans".

Ilse's parents joined other workers in demonstrations against Hitler's takeover of power. When Hitler ordered the burning of "un-German" books, they buried their own copies in their garden. And they continued to discuss politics with trusted friends in their own houses or at lake-side cafés at the weekends. But Ilse was too young to worry about any of these things.

By 1940 Ilse was old enough to go to a meeting of the Hitler Youth. Her grandmother on her mother's side bought her the uniform – black skirt, white blouse, black scarf and brown leather scarf toggle. There was a ceremony at which Ilse and the other new members took an oath of loyalty to Hitler before the Nazi flag and formally received landing. Nonsense! As if enemy planes could ever get to Berlin. . . . But then we have a 'real' alarm and they are a bit upset because the first bombs have fallen. (Ilse Koehn, *Mischling Second Degree*, Hamish Hamilton, 1977)

The bombing had started, so Ilse was sent away, to Radoczowitz, wherever that was. At the station in Berlin the children were sent off with banners and a band. Twenty-four hours later they were in Czechoslovakia, tramping through a dripping forest, with Czech partisans shooting over their heads from out of the gloom. Finally they arrived at an old hotel which had been taken over by the German occupation forces. Even though the Hitler Youth leaders did not dare to take them outside the grounds of the hotel, they were told to write cheerful letters home to keep their parents happy.

The time passed. There were uniform inspections and room inspections. There were also games and songs. But there were no regular lessons. The evacuated teachers were

60 You too can help!

61 Sudeten Germans greet their "liberators".

back their scarves and toggles. She went to one more meeting and then stayed away. No one seemed to be bothered very much.

1940 was a year of victories for Germany. This made it the year of private trading in Luebars, the village outside Berlin where Ilse was living with Grandmother Dereck:

Grossmutter [Grandmother] barters her preserves, fruit, eggs for things that come from the invaded countries. A pair of shoes for Mutti [Mother] from Prague, soap from Belgium, silk from France. There are men from our neighbourhood in all these places, and they send things home, where their wives and mothers trade over the back-garden fences. That's also where the women vent their anger against air-raid drills and the new laws that require a pail of water or sand on every stair as bored and confused as their evacuated pupils. In September 1941 they were all sent back to Berlin. There were no banners and no bands, but at least it was home and Ilse's mother was there to meet her. She had a few hours off from her new job in a railway ticket office. Ilse's father, who had been working non-stop for 24 hours, repairing a cable ruptured by an Allied air-raid, was asleep. When he woke a few hours later:

. . . he says that "we Germans" have done terrible things in Poland and Czechoslovakia . . . "Ernst!" Oma [Grandma] interrupts, "Is this necessary?" "Yes, it is," Vati retorts angrily. "It is indeed. I want Ilse to know why all Germans, anything German, will soon be something hateful and despicable to the rest of the world".

Vati then produced a radio. Crouched under a blanket to deaden the sound, the family listened to the BBC:

"This man, in far-away London, talks about German troops retreating from Moscow, Leningrad, of General Rommel being beaten in North Africa. He names specific army units, commanders, places that our "victorious armies" have abandoned.

Ilse was astonished and frightened – and interested.

In the summer of 1942 Ilse went away with school friends to the Baltic island of Ruegen to help with farm work. She thought it would be fun to go away with her friends, but it wasn't fun. It was very hard work – sorting through rotten potatoes, hoeing turnips and picking berries. There were the usual Hitler Youth slogans to spur them on:

It's not shameful to fall, only to stay down.
Tough as leather, hard as steel, swift as greyhounds.
The German woman doesn't drink, doesn't smoke, doesn't paint herself.

But most of the time they were too tired to be spurred on.

After a few months back in Berlin, Ilse was evacuated again with 175 other girls from her school and five teachers. They went to a mountain district, far from Berlin – the village of Harrachsdorf, a resort full of hotels, crowded with children and wounded soldiers. Helga and Irene, Hitler Youth leaders were assigned to supervise the girls' discipline and morale:

They demonstrate how towels should hang, both ends exactly equal; they fold and refold garments, show how it's done. Toothbrushes have to stand at attention. That is, they have to stand at a certain angle in their glasses. The worst is over. We get a two rating. Considering that one is best and six worst, two isn't bad. A rating of six gets you a week of potato-peeling and/or kitchen duty. The way Helga and Irene inspect, there won't be any need for volunteers for a long time to come.

Once again there were parades, songs and games but few regular lessons. The main event of every day was the radio news bulletin:

Our only interest is to hear whether Berlin has been bombed . . . the newscasts never tell us what we want to hear; which section of town has been hit. It's always "The enemy attacked the nation's capital today, directing their attack mainly at residential sectors. The enemy has sustained heavy losses; thirty-two planes have been shot down, – while we lost none." You can get a pretty good idea, though, how heavy the air-raid was by how many planes were shot down. Tonight there is a change in the standard phrasing. For the first time we have not "taken victoriously" yet another Russian town. Instead, our forces make an "orderly retreat" for the purpose of straightening our front line.

The girls had a room-decorating contest; they learned to ski in winter; they went climbing and swimming in summer; they produced their own hand-written newspaper. In March 1943 Ilse got a letter from her father. There

62 An idealized Aryan maiden appeals for funds to ▷ build youth hostels and cabins.

was a cross at the bottom. This was a special code between her and her father and she knew that Oma, her Jewish grandmother, was dead. Six SS men had arrived in the middle of the night and looted her flat. At dawn she went to the railway station. She died, aged 84, soon after arriving in Theresienstadt concentration camp.

In June 1944 Ilse's father visited her. She was overjoyed to see him but had to confess that she was shortly to be made a leader in the Hitler Youth:

"You must, under all circumstances, avoid it. I don't know how, but do it you must. Promise me." We look each other in the eye. I know he knows that it's not going to be easy.

63 Winter (left) and summer (centre and right) uniforms of the League of German Girls.

Bundestracht des BDM.

Untergauführerin
des BDM.
in der allgemeinen
Wintertracht

Jungmädel
in der allgemeinen
Sommertracht

Untergauführerin
des BDM.
in der allgemeinen
Sommertracht

"The war is not going well. No one knows what will happen." His voice becomes a whisper. "You do know that I and your whole family are opposed to Hitler. You will, of course, not mention this to anyone. I mean *anyone*, not even to your very best friend."

By August 1944 Germany was being pressed from all sides and the government declared a state of total war. Boys aged 15 to 18 and men from 50 to 60 were called up. "Mischlings, first degree", were rounded up by the SS. This included Ilse's father, who was sent to help build a new airport. Ilse knew nothing of this, but she, too, was called to work, helping an old woman bring in her hay harvest. In September 1944 Ilse was sent to a training camp for youth leaders. She remembered her father's warning and cried. But she had to go. The camp was in a beautiful house, where the 20 chosen girls were waited on by Czech maids. There was no drill and very little propaganda. Almost all the time was spent on music and crafts – painting, drawing, poetry, acting, puppetry and toy-making. But Ilse was afraid she would be awarded a leader's cord. Instead the camp organizers thought she was so good that they would recommend her for further training. But the next course never took place. By October 1944 the Allies were on German soil. And the Russians were closing in on Prague, 80 kilometres to the south-west of the girls' camp.

Then, without warning, Ilse's father turned up to take her away. He didn't have permission, he didn't have the right papers. She never knew how he got there. He was just there and told her quietly to slip away after dinner. So she packed a small bag, threw it out through a window and jumped out after it into the snow. Her father took her all the way to the suburbs of Berlin and then went back to the airport site he was working on. An SS firing squad was waiting for him but an air-raid had damaged important cables and he was needed to repair them. His execution was postponed, indefinitely.

Back with her grandparents, Ilse learned that only three things were important – living through the daily air-raids, killing the pig they had raised and what they would do when the Russians came. When the pig was killed it weighed over 300 kilos. The family was allowed to keep a third, the rest went to the state. Nothing was wasted. What couldn't be cured as bacon was made into sausages or lard. The raids continued, day and night, with no anti-aircraft fire to oppose them:

. . . yet, surprisingly, the city still functions. Gas, water, electricity all work, except for short periods when one of the main lines is hit. Trains run, though with enormous delays. People go to work. The radio blares daily messages that those found guilty of leaving their assigned posts will be court-martialed.

On 18 April 1945 Russian troops began fighting their way through the outskirts of Berlin itself. The following day Ilse's mother walked home to Luebars from work in central Berlin, a six hour journey:

"It was madness, absolute madness. Thousands of people at the station . . . You can't imagine the chaos! Soldiers and civilians carrying what looked like whole households. SS . . . still checking papers, grabbing men and marching them off to be shot. Everyone shouting, screaming, pushing, yelling above the gun-fire – and I'm still selling tickets and don't even know whether there are still trains."

An advance guard of Russians arrived in Luebars the following day. They set up gun-sites, laid down field telephones lines and ordered all local shopkeepers to sell off their supplies of food. When the main army began to arrive a day later the soldiers looted houses as they passed through. Ilse and her mother hid underneath the floor of the house for three days and nights until her grandparents told her it was safe to come out. Then they hid in a

64   "Liberated!".

loft above the pigsty in the garden for another four days and nights. Still the massive Russian army rumbled past their house. Finally, on the tenth day, grandmother came to let them out for a breath of fresh air:

"Everyone has survived. . . . They threatened to shoot Grossvater [Grandfather] a couple of times because he didn't have a watch. . . . Do you know that at one point I counted three-hundred and fourteen Russians in our small house? Three-hundred and fourteen! They made me cook for them. One of them gave me half a loaf of bread. You wouldn't think so, but they really have nothing to eat themselves. . . . The chairs and table are broken . . . and almost all the glasses and dishes and all the pictures are smashed. . . . Wait till you see the cellar! . . . What a mess! All the cider bottles broken too.

Smashed them when they were looking for schnapps. Thank God we didn't have any. They were drunk enough as it was."

Germany surrendered on 7 May but on the 22nd Ilse and her mother were still in hiding. The war ended for them on that day, when Ilse's father came to collect them. He had escaped from the airport construction site more than a month before. Germany was now divided but at least Ilse's family was reunited.

(After the war Ilse Koehn trained as a graphic artist. In 1958 she emigrated to America, where she still lives. Initially she worked in advertising and exhibited her paintings, and eventually became a book illustrator and designer. Her autobiography *Mischling, Second Degree* was published in 1977 by Hamish Hamilton.)

GLOSSARY

Abwehr German military counter-intelligence, headed by Admiral Canaris.

Alte Kämpfer "Old Fighters", early members of the Nazi Party.

Aryan Member of the most superior racial group in the Nazi hierarchy of human types. The term originally applied to a group of North Indian languages from which many European languages (including German and English) have evolved. Later the term was applied to the speakers of those languages, who were supposed to have been an ancient warrior-race of outstanding beauty and intelligence. They were considered the original creators of the world's great achievements, including European and, therefore, German civilization. The language link is borne out by historical evidence, but the notion of a heroic "master-race" has no scientific foundation.

Austlandsdeutsche Germans living outside German territory.

Autobahn Motorway.

Blitzkrieg "Lightning war"; method of warfare depending on close co-ordination of air-power and mechanized forces to accomplish speedy destruction of an enemy's forces.

Deutsche Arbeitsfront (DAF) German Labour Front; Nazi-controlled trade-union organization intended to control workers by superseding free unions and regulating welfare.

Endlösung The "Final Solution"; the code word for the extermination of the Jews.

Final Solution See Endlösung.

Freikorps "Free Corps", bands of ex-soldiers prominent in political turmoil after the Great War. Most opposed Communism and border pressures from French, Poles and other neighbouring powers.

Führer, Der "The Leader" – Hitler, who came to combine the offices of Head of Government (Chancellor) and the Head of State (President).

Führerprinzip "Leader principle"; the basis of decision-making in the Nazi theory of the state. Democracy, government by the active consent of the governed, was to be replaced by a pyramid of leaders, each with absolute authority over those below him and owing absolute obedience to those above him. At the top of the pyramid would be the supreme leader, Hitler.

Gauleiter Regional head of Nazi party organization; his actual power depended on a combination of personality and circumstance.

German Christian Movement "Deutsche Christian"; a Nazi-sponsored minority group aiming to take control of the Protestant churches by gaining key appointments. Opposed by the Pfarrernotbunt organized by Niemöller and the Confessional or Spiritual Church represented by such dissidents as Bonhoeffer.

Gestapo Abbreviation for "Geheime Staatspolizei", Secret State Police; the most feared of the Nazi security services, able to act virtually outside the law.

Gleichschaltung "Co-ordination" or "streamlining"; short-hand term for the Nazification of all German institutions after 1933.

Grand Alliance Term favoured by Churchill to describe the anti-Nazi coalition of the UK, USA and USSR. F.D. Roosevelt preferred the term "United Nations".

Herrenvolk "Master-race", i.e. Germans and other "Aryans".

Kraft durch Freude "Strength through joy"; Nazi leisure organization controlled by the DAF.

Lebensraum "Living-space"; code word for German policy of expanding territories at the expense of neighbouring states.

Luftwaffe "Air weapon"; German air force; rebuilt by Goering in the 1930s, it failed to win air supremacy over Britain or to prevent long-range bombing of Germany.

Mischling Nazi classification for a person of part Jewish descent.

NSDAP (Nationalsozialistische Deutsche Arbeiter-partei) National Socialist German Workers' Party; full name of Nazi Party.

New Order Hitler's vision of a Europe dominated by a Nazi "Herrenvolk" in which Slavs and other "non-aryans" would serve only as slave labourers and Jews would be eliminated.

Nuremberg Laws Racist legislation promulgated in 1935 which banned Jews from public office and deprived them of many other civil rights. They also made the swastika (*Hakenleruz*) and official emblem of the state.

Nuremberg Trials Trials of 24 major Nazi leaders before an international military tribunal sitting at Nürmburg (Nuremberg) 20 November 1945 – 31 August 1946. Twelve were sentenced to death, three acquitted and the rest imprisoned for various terms. Further war criminals' trials were held during the Allied occupation of Germany and afterwards in both West and East Germany, as well as in the USSR.

OKW (Oberkommando der Wehrmacht) High Command of the Armed Forces.

Ordensburg Schools Military-style training camps where selected teenagers would undergo rigorous physical and academic education to prepare them for future leadership roles.

Panzer Armour, armoured formations.

Pogrom (Russian: "devastation"); anti-Jewish riot or massacre, common in Tzarist Russia in the 1880s.

Pour le Mérite Highest German award for valour in the Great War.

Putsch (literally: "revolt"); attempt to seize control of the Government by violence.

Reichstag Parliament, a virtually meaningless institution during the period of Nazi rule, maintained as a device for granting privileges to Nazi leaders and as a forum for propaganda.

SA (Sturmabteilungen) Stormtroopers or "Brown-shirts", established in 1921 by Ernst Röhm as the private army of the Nazi party.

SD (Sicherheitsdienst) Security service of the SS, established in 1932 and developed by Heydrich as the main security service of the Nazi Party.

SS (Schutz-staffel) Hitler's bodyguard squad, established 1928, and expanded by Himmler into a massive, privileged state-within-the-state.

Third Reich (Third Realm) Term used to describe the Nazi regime (1933-45) which was intended to be a "Thousand Year Reich". The first Reich was reckoned to be the Holy Roman Empire (800 – 1806) and the second the Germany of 1871 – 1918.

Vergeltungswaffen "Revenge weapons"; the rocket-bomb V2 used against Britain in 1944.

Volkische Beobachter *Racial Observer*: semi official Nazi Party newspaper, edited by Julius Streicher.

Volkssturm German Home Guard.

Volkswagen "People's car", never actually mass-produced.

Waffen SS Armed units of SS.

Wehrmacht German armed forces, as distinct from the Waffen SS.

Werewolves 12 to 14 year-old boys drafted into army for last-ditch defence of Germany.

Weimar Republic Democratic regime which ruled Germany 1919-33 under a liberal parliamentary constitution drawn up in the city of Weimar. In the eyes of many Germans it was tainted by its acceptance of the Versailles Peace Treaty which ended the Great War and acknowledged Germany's guilt in starting it.

DATE LIST

1918
9 November — Abdication of Kaiser Wilhelm II: proclamation of a republic.
11 November — Armistice ends Great War.

1919
28 June — Germany signs Treaty of Versailles.
16 September — Hitler joins German Workers' Party.

1920
24 February — Hitler proclaims 25-point programme of the National Socialist German Workers' Party.

1921
3 August — Formation of the SA.

1923
11 January — French troops occupy Ruhr industrial area.
8-9 November — Abortive Hitler putsch in Munich.
23 November — Nazi Party banned.

1924
1 April — Hitler condemned to five years' imprisonment (released 20 December).
9 April — Dawes Plan stabilizes German economy.

1925
27 February — Nazi Party refounded.
9 November — Formation of the SS.

1926
8 September — Germany joins League of Nations.

1929
24 October — Wall Street stock market crash.

1930
14 September — Nazi Party increases Reichstag seats from 12 to 107.

1931
11 May — Crisis of German banking system.

1932
25 February — Hitler becomes a German citizen.
3 March and 10 April — Hitler defeated by Hindenburg in two-stage election for President.
13 April — SA and SS banned (ban lifted 14 June).
31 July — Nazi Party wins 230 out of 608 seats in Reichstag.

13 August — Hindenburg refuses to appoint Hitler as Chancellor.
6 November — Nazi Party seats fall from 230 to 196 in Reichstag elections.

1933
30 January — Hitler appointed Chancellor.
27 February — Reichstag fire is followed by suspension of civil rights.
5 March — Last multi-party Reichstag elections. Nazi Party wins 288 seats (44 per cent).
24 March — Enabling Law grants Hitler dictatorial powers for four years.

1933
1 April — Boycott of Jewish shops and services throughout Germany.
2 May — Trade unions banned.
14 July — Nazi Party declared the only legal political party.
20 July — Hitler signs Concordat with Vatican.
22 September — Reich Chamber of Culture established under Goebbels' direction. Burning of books begins.
4 October — Authors Law controls permission to write and publish.
19 October — Germany leaves the League of Nations.

1934
30 June — Night of the Long Knives – purge of the SA.
2 August — Death of President Hindenberg. Hitler proclaims his succession as head of state and of government. Army takes personal oath of loyalty to the Führer.
24 October — German Labour Front established as Nazi-sponsored union movement.

1935
16 March — Reintroduction of universal conscription.
15 September — Anti-Jewish "Nuremberg Laws" proclaimed at party rally.

1936
7 March — Reoccupation of demilitarized Rhineland.
July-August — Olympic Games held in Berlin.

1937
6 November — Anti-Comintern Pact with Italy.

1938

4 February	Hitler becomes Commander-in-Chief of the armed forces.
12-13 March	Anschluss – Nazi occupation of Austria.
29 September	Munich agreement leads to German annexation of Sudetenland.
9 November	Reichskristallnacht – Pogrom against Jews throughout Germany.

1939

15 March	German troops occupy Bohemia and Moravia.
24 August	Nazi-Soviet pact signed.
1 September	German troops attack Poland – outbreak of Second World War.
3 September	Britain and France declare war on Germany.
1 October	End of organized Polish resistance.

1940

9 April	German invasion of Denmark and Norway.
10 May	German attack on Holland, Belgium, France and Luxemburg.
27 May – 4 June	Evacuation of British Expeditionary Force. from Dunkirk.
22 June	French sign armistice with Germany.

1941

22 June	German attack on Soviet Union.
11 December	Germany declares war on the United States.

1942

20 January	Administration of the "Final Solution" of the "Jewish Question" is entrusted to Adolf Eichmann.
23 October – 4 November	Battle of El Alamein.

1943

30 January	German surrender at Stalingrad.
11 June	Himmler orders destruction of the Jewish ghettoes.
25 July	Fall of Mussolini.
3 September	Allied invasion of Italy.
8 September	Surrender of Italy to the Allies.

1944

6 June	Allied invasion of Normandy.
20 July	Stauffenberg attempts assassination of Hitler.

1945

30 April	Hitler commits suicide in Berlin.
7 May	Unconditional surrender of Germany.

BIOGRAPHICAL NOTES

Adenauer, Konrad (1876-1967). A consistent anti-Nazi, he served as Chancellor of the German Federal Republic 1949-63 and was thus chiefly responsible for the re-establishment of democracy in post-war Germany.

Amann, Max (1891-1957). Hitler's Great War sergeant who dominated the press and publishing under the Nazis, enormously enriching himself and Hitler in the process.

Baeck, Leo (1873-1956). Leading rabbi of the Jewish community in Germany under the Nazis, he miraculously survived Theresienstadt concentration camp.

Bormann, Martin (1900-?). Head of the Nazi party organization and personal assistant to Hitler, whom he relieved of most routine administration. His precise fate is not known.

Braun, Eva (1912-1945). Hitler's mistress from 1932 and his wife for the last few hours of his life. A pretty, vacuous and non-political figure.

Braun, Wernher von (1912-77). Engineer who developed the V2 rocket used against England and later took a leading part in the US space programme.

Canaris, Wilhelm (1887-1945). Head of the Abwehr 1935-44, who both supported Hitler's policies and plotted his death; he was executed in 1945.

Dietrich, Sepp (1892-1966). Commander of Hitler's bodyguard, murderer of Ernst Röhm and one of the few early Nazis to become a competent military leader. Imprisoned for ten years for massacring American POWs.

Doenitz, Karl (1891-1980). Creator of Germany's submarine fleet, Commander-in-Chief of the Navy from 1943 and Hitler's designated successor.

Drexler, Anton (1884-1942). Co-founder of the Nazi party and co-author of its 25-point programme; ousted by Hitler in 1921. Died in obscurity.

Eichmann, Adolf (1906-62). SS Chief of the Jewish Office of the Gestapo with major administrative responsibility for organizing the "Final Solution". Abducted from Argentina by Israeli agents, tried and executed in Jerusalem.

Flick, Friedrich (1883-1972). Industrialist and Nazi supporter whose war-time industrial empire made extensive use of forced labour. Imprisoned 1947-51, he rebuilt his fortune, leaving a billion dollars to his playboy son and nothing to his victims.

Frank, Hans (1900-46), Hitler's personal lawyer and Governor-General of Nazi-occupied Poland, who confessed his guilt, condemned Hitler, was reconciled to the Catholic Church and executed as a war criminal.

Funk, Walther (1890-1970). Leading contact man between the Nazi party and its big business supporters.

Galen, Clemens August Graf von (1878-1946). Cardinal Archbishop of Münster who defended Christianity against Nazi paganism, preached successfully against the SS euthanasia programme and survived Sachsenhausen concentration camp.

Goerdeler, Carl (1884-1945). Civilian leader of German resistance, executed after being implicated in the July 1944 plot which, if it had succeeded, would have made him Chancellor of Germany.

Goering, Hermann (1893-1946). Great War fighter ace, head of the Luftwaffe, morphine addict, art collector and founder of the Gestapo. Lost influence after the failure of the Luftwaffe to win air supremacy over Britain and committed suicide two hours before his scheduled hanging at Nuremberg.

Grüber, Heinrich (1891-1975). Protestant churchman who risked his life to save Jews from Nazi persecution, survived three years in concentration camps and campaigned after the war to remind all Germans of their moral obligations to the Jews and to warn against Neo-Nazism.

Guderian, Heinz (1888-1954). Expert in tank warfare and architect of the Blitzkrieg campaigns against Poland, France and the USSR.

Hess, Rudolf (1894-). Deputy leader of the Nazi party who parachuted into Scotland on a personal peace initiative in 1941, was arrested and remains imprisoned at Spandau.

Hoffmann, Heinrich (1885-1957). Hitler's official photographer who took 2½ million pictures of the Führer.

Jodl, Alfred (1890-1946). Hitler's closest military adviser, executed for war crimes and posthumously exonerated by a German de-Nazification court.

Koch, Ilse (1907-67). Wife of the commandant of Buchenwald concentration camp, renowned for her personal sadism. Committed suicide in prison.

Krupp von Bohlen und Halbach, Gustav (1878-1950). Armaments manufacturer who, with his son Alfred (1907-67) helped supply the Nazi war machine.

Mengele, Josef (1911-). Chief doctor at Auschwitz who organized medical experiments on the inmates. Escaped to Paraguay.

Papen, Franz von (1879-1969). Reich Chancellor in 1932, Hitler's Deputy Chancellor until July 1934 and thereafter a useful nonentity.

Reitsch, Hanna (1912-79). Outstanding female test pilot and personal favourite and fervent admirer of Hitler.

Ribbentrop, Joachim von (1893-1946). Nazi Minister of

Foreign Affairs 1938-45 who steadily lost influence with the outbreak of war. Hanged at Nuremberg for war crimes.

Röhm, Ernst (1887-1934). Brutal, homosexual head of the SA, who threatened to rival Hitler's own power and was murdered in the "Night of the Long Knives" (30 June 1934).

Rosenberg, Alfred (1893-1946). Semi-official philosopher of Nazism who developed its racial and cultural theories but exerted little real influence on policy. Hanged at Nuremberg.

Sauckel, Fritz (1894-1946). Plenipotentiary-General for Labour Mobilization 1942-5, who organized the deportation of 5 million people from occupied territories to work as slave labourers in Germany. Hanged at Nuremberg.

Schacht, Hjalmar (1877-1970). Financier who organized the funding of German re-armament, was disillusioned with Nazism and became implicated in the resistance. Released from Flossenburg and ultimately cleared of all charges.

Schirach, Baldur von (1907-74). Leader of German youth movement and war-time Governor of Vienna, who served 20 years in Spandau and tried in his memoirs to atone for his past.

Scholtz-Klink, Gertrud (1902-). Leader of the Nazi Women's League which promoted the cult of housework and child-rearing for the glory of the Reich. Acquitted of major war crimes.

Skorzeny, Otto (1908-75). Daring commando leader who rescued Mussolini from captivity, was acquitted of war crimes and in the post-war period helped organize the escape from Europe of ex-members of the SS via Spain.

Strasser, Gregor (1892-1934). A serious rival to Hitler in the early days of Nazism, advocating revolutionary social policies. Murdered in the "Night of the Long Knives" (1934).

Streicher, Julius (1885-1946). Rabble-rousing anti-Semite and editor of the viciously racist *Der Stürmer* (1923-45). Ousted from his party posts in 1940 after insulting Goering. Hanged at Nuremberg.

Thaelmann, Ernst (1886-1944). Communist party leader, imprisoned after the Reichstag fire (February 1933) and murdered in Buchenwald.

Thyssen, Fritz (1873-1951). Industrialist and early supporter of Hitler. Disillusioned by Nazi persecution of Catholics and Jews, he fled abroad, was returned by Vichy police and sat out the war in prison.

Ulbricht, Walter (1893-1973). Communist leader who fled Germany in 1933. Effective creator of the post-war German Democratic Republic (East Germany).

Wagner, Winifred (1897-1980). English daughter-in-law of the composer Richard Wagner whose music was Hitler's passion. A close personal friend of the Führer, she organized the annual Bayreuth Festival until the fall of the Third Reich.

Wiener, Alfred (1885-1964). Secretary of the largest Jewish organization in Germany until 1933, he devoted his later life to documenting Nazi activities. The Wiener Library he created in London helped British war-time propaganda and the prosecution of war criminals as well as remaining a major archive for scholars.

BOOKS FOR FURTHER READING

Karl Bracher, *The German Dictatorship* (Penguin, 1978)

Alan Bullock, *Hitler: A Study in Tyranny* (Penguin, 1962)

Lucy Dawidowicz, *The War Against the Jews 1933-45* (Penguin, 1977)

Joachim C. Fest, *The Face of the Third Reich* (Penguin, 1978)

Joachim C. Fest, *Hitler* (Penguin, 1977)

G.S. Gruber, *History of the SS* (Granada, 1982)

Richard Grunberger, *A Social History of the Third Reich* (Penguin, 1974)

Wieslaw Kielar, *Anus Mundi: Five Years in Auschwitz* (Penguin, 1982)

W. Laqueur, *The Terrible Secret (Penguin, 1982)*

George L. Mosse, *Nazism* (Blackwell, 1978)

Albert Speer, *Inside the Third Reich* (Sphere, 1971)

Albert Speer, *The Slave State* (Weidenfeld & Nicolson, 1981)

William L. Shirer, *The Rise & Fall of the Third Reich* (Pan, 1964)

Simon Taylor, *Germany 1918-33* (Duckworth, 1983)

INDEX